Nancy Phelan was born lived in England for a nt travelled widely in the Pacif East and the Middle East USSR. She was Visual Aids Officer of the South Pacific Commission for five years and has published six travel books, four novels, two books of autobiography and a biography of Charles Mackerras. She has also collaborated on a Russian cook book and a number of books on Hatha Yoga. She lives partly in Sydney and partly in an historic gatehouse in the Blue Mountains.

IMPRINT

A KINGDOM BY THE SEA

NANCY PHELAN

ANGUS
& ROBERTSON
PUBLISHERS

For Sheila,
and in memory of John

IMPRINT

ANGUS & ROBERTSON PUBLISHERS

First published in 1969 by Angus & Robertson Publishers,
Unit 4, Eden Park, 31 Waterloo Road, North Ryde, NSW, Australia 2113;
and 16 Golden Square, London W1R 4BN, United Kingdom
First published in paperback 1980
First published in Imprint 1990

Copyright © Nancy Phelan 1969

National Library of Australia
Cataloguing-in-publication data:

Phelan, Nancy, 1913-
A kingdom by the sea.
ISBN 0 207 16611 0.
I. Title.
A823'.3

Printed by Globe Press, Victoria

Cover illustration: *Balmoral*, 1927, by Roy de Maistre
Private Collection

CONTENTS

1	The Bay	1
2	Parents	8
3	Jemima	15
4	A Flight of Parakeets	25
5	It was the Music	36
6	Killarney	45
7	Salt Horse and Sea Biscuits	52
8	A Little Bit of Sauce-a	60
9	Dipping In and Dipping Out	68
10	Parties	77
11	Poor Henry	84
12	The Scarlet Letter	92
13	Carpentry	101
14	Night on the Harbour	116
15	Lady Authoress	122
16	Holidays	133
17	The Warren	142
18	One Summer Night	153
19	No Trespassers	158
20	Sunrise	166

ACKNOWLEDGEMENTS

I should like to thank my sister, Sheila Smith White, and my cousin, Judge J. E. H. Pilcher, for helping with family reminiscences.

N.P.

I

The Bay

In the days of my parents' marriage the hill where I grew up was mainly bush, the setting for picnics and vigorous walks. The narrow strait at The Spit was crossed by a groaning punt on a wire. By the time I was born houses were forming themselves into streets along the ridge, but gardens were still large, the nights undisturbed by Sydney's traffic.

From every window we could see the bay, sleek, smooth, brimming, at high tide its white beaches half-sheeted with glass, rocks submerged, gold-walled caves turned to shadowed pools. Far out, North Head rose from a dreaming ocean, glazed with sun. In the foreground the lighthouse on Grotto Point looked down at itself in a still sea, clear in the hot unmoving air.

At intervals Manly ferries crossed the open space between the Heads, by night diamond bracelets set with emerald and ruby. In calm weather they steamed majestically, in storms rose and vanished behind immense waves. Only rarely, in extreme tempests, did they fail to appear.

On fine weekend mornings a butterfly armada set out, delicate, darting; in the richer afternoon light, when the wind had dropped, the procession returned, sweeping in, faintly vibrating, clusters of towed boats strung out where chilled figures took in sails and prepared for the moorings. Across the bay's entrance gothic sails stood in rows, like white painted moths.

Top-heavy launches followed the races, crowded with people and beer, and on week days small black *Victoria and Albert* steamers with rakish smoke-stacks fussed in, with public servants on board, or strange schooners and lines of barges made a silent mysterious progress up towards Powderworks Bay, in the forbidden far reaches of Middle Harbour.

The bay was always beautiful, mutable, strange; yet I see it only, in childhood, under the pale Greek exhausted sky of summer, the water dovetailed serenely into the caves and rocks.

We told the tide by these rocks, looking out from the balcony. If they were invisible you ran down the hill to the beach, for it meant that the pool would be full; if they were exposed it was not worthwhile, for to swim in The Open was forbidden.

Yet it was into the shark-infested Open that my father dropped us as infants, while my mother wailed on the sand. He believed that babies, being animals, swim by instinct and it was imperative we swim as soon as possible so we could go out in the boat. My mother protested only on grounds of health. Unnautical, docile, devoted, she had learnt to regard sailing as a basic essential, like sleep, eating, music and books.

There was no gradual waking-up in those days; you opened your eyes and were at once alive in every sense. Sometimes I got up immediately; sometimes lay watching the light. Rising suns flashed straight through the eastern windows and struck the wall by my bed, slow pale fingers, stiffly spread, moving up the wall, pushing through the dusk, thrusting aside the night. The strange inevitable movement, the faint inexorable quality of the light brought a happiness untouched by the puzzling sadness that so often accompanied beauty.

When the pallid fingers had driven the dark away and the wall blazed with morning I would lie thinking blissfully of the day ahead, of long radiant hours unmarked by signposts of time; and beyond that, another day, and still another, stretching on and on, always the same, all golden, uncharted, saturated with sun.

From the open dew-beaded balcony outside my room you could watch the light down in the garden, sifting through leaves, striking webs of seed-pearls hung in air, casting shadows at the feet of hollyhocks. Scents rose, nocturnal still, with all the cool reserve of flowers at night. Briefly there was suspension, a breath held. Never again would this moment come, never quite the same, no matter how often. . . . Then the light strengthened, glinting through tree-trunks. Shadows became sharp, the tops of trees, lit with yellow, were outlined against glittering water, all greens intensified—cypress, poplar, eucalyptus, willow, pittosporum, wattle, Moreton Bay. The garden's slow subtle abandonment to growing warmth began, the generous giving-out from softening petals. The thick springy grass sparkled. I knew how it felt beneath bare feet.

Sometimes there was a different movement in the garden: my mother, in kimono, under the cypresses, a hopeful spaniel rump beside her, bending to see if seedlings had survived snails, inhaling her scented bouvardia. This was another kind of pleasure, it meant food and company were at hand. Soon I could sit on the kitchen table in my nightgown, eating bread and jam, feeling the day had started, or go to the piano, forbidden while others slept, racing my brother while our mother cried we would be late for school.

In summer holidays one stepped straight from bed into a swimming costume and ran down the hill through warm cicada-shaken air, into the water. The exhilaration of this pulsating background, the morning scents, the awareness of great heat to come was heightened by still-sleeping houses all round, by having the world to oneself. On the damp untouched beach the fine white sand squeaked beneath my feet. I was the first to step upon this new-created earth, the first to float in these shallows with the rising sun on my face.

Learning to swim, like learning to read, increased independence. With books you did not need people; being able to swim allowed you to go to the beach without adults. In return, it was only fair not to mention near-drownings, falls from cliffs, streaming gashes on rocks. Sometimes our activities were reported by interested neighbours—swimming too far out in The Open, smoking in caves, stealing fruit, trespassing, insulting property-owners, climbing prohibited heights, getting cut off by the tide. Torn by oyster-shells, sunburnt, powdered with dried salt we returned home at dusk, too tired for speech, and fell into bed immediately after dinner.

Anything served for excitement . . . a dead dog in a sack fished from the water, sharks' eggs, French-letters washed up by the tide, jumping on frizzled sea-weed to make it pop, running with screams from a bearded cave-man who lived round the rocks. Such encounters were not referred to at home, nor the strange men who sometimes at dusk slipped out from bushes wearing only a hat. Though my mother seemed not to fear we would drown or die of tetanus she often, with embarrassment, warned us against Nasty Men who offered sweets to little girls coming home from school. If she had known our secluded beach was a favorite resort of exhibitionists we should not have been allowed there alone.

We kept quiet, even to each other, about these evening primroses, secretly frightened, ashamed of our fears. It was not the grotesque performance so much as the suddenness, the utter silence that chilled; such a chill as descended when, ankle-deep in The Open, you saw a dark shadow, a triangular fin cruise soundlessly through water you had just left.

But since rational fear of sharks, intuitive fear of perverts were less than fear of lost liberty, we rewarded our parents' trust with deception, coated over with professional innocence; fake innocence, childhood's defence against adults, essential weapon for life in Occupied Territory.

As with sharks and Nasty Men, so in other matters.

"Go on, Nancy. You go and get us some Cappos."

I was always the one sent to buy cigarettes. Pink-and-white, fair hair streaming, wide-eyed and innocent I stood at the counter.

"Please, Daddy says—can-I-have-a-packet-of-cigarettes?"

4

"What sort, dear?"

An embarrassed blush; a helpless glance; a faintly apologetic murmur: "I can't remember the name. . . . Something like Captain?"

"Do you think it might be Capstan, dear?"

Holding in readiness the exact amount, the savings of many days, I would say uncertainly, "Yes, I think so. How much are they? Oh, I do hope he gave me enough."

We were crafty about choosing shops. Too close to home, they might learn my father never smoked cigarettes; patronized too often, they might suspect my chronically failing memory.

Smoking took place under the house or in a secluded cave in the gully—when not on the beach we spent much time in cellars and caves—and was followed by ritual chewing of nasturtium or gum leaves.

"John, have you been smoking?"

"No, mum."

"Are you sure?"

"Yes, mum."

"Let me smell your breath."

We viewed her with pity, poor innocent, as she sniffed at our eucalyptoid blasts. Suspicious, unconvinced, without proof she would try to extract the truth from our eyes. Bland, glassy as fish we gazed back.

We lied and deceived not for villainy but to preserve independence. Though deprived of Child Experts to uplift, analyse, investigate, classify, improve, understand and explain us to ourselves we still had to fight for privacy on our own terms, for a world of our own from which to emerge, when necessary, to meet adults on neutral ground. Our leisure must be free for making investigations and experiments with life, sex, danger, violence; for activities forbidden by parents; for fighting, for being cruel and anti-social and beastly; for blissfully being ourselves, in our own right, as distinct from somebody's children.

5

Now that the old house is in other hands and only my sister and I are left, that life has become a dream; yet a dream so vivid that smallest details linger and sensations are as fresh as in that very time.

Though the bay remains, all else is changed, the scene shifted, main characters, even background and bystanders gone. Where are those tough little furry-faced boys called Ernie and Ray, with felt hats and braces and heavy tweed shorts made from their fathers' trousers? Those little albino mosquito girls in lettuce-green organdie, with immense bows on their straight white hair and heart-and-chain bracelets on thin speckled arms? The Mad Boys, like Mad Vivvy down at the lighthouse, who drooled and held his limp hands like flippers and stumbled over his feet? The Saturday drunks wedded to lobsters and bags of prawns?

Down on the beach strange families lived in canvas houses dug into the dunes. Women screamed in the night and purple-faced bookies zigzagged down the hill with suitcases bulging with grog. Across the water the hills above Castle Rock and Clontarf were untouched; trams groaned and lurched down an unsurfaced Parrawi Road and the street to Chinaman's Beach was an overgrown track.

Round the rocks were other beaches, exciting in foreignness, backed by lush jungle growths. Among dark lilli-pilli trees monkey-vines twisted and swayed, strong enough to swing upon; water trickled among moist fungoid growths, smells of rotting leaves and wood rose when feet slipped in slime. Accessible only at low tide, these beaches were spiced with danger. High tide submerged them. From behind came the threat of landslides, clay and rocks slithering down after rain. No paths, no steps existed. Far above, in another world, the Spit tram rocked and bucketed along the ridge, its overhead pole crashing down as it flung itself round curves.

It is different now. The Mad Vivvies, Rays and Ernies, albino mosquitoes and prawn-loving drunks have been tidied up. TV stars have moved in, TV antennae grid-iron the sky.

6

Where camp-dwellers lusted and fought, desirable-residences stand among triple garages and swimming-pools. Landslides have been restrained, roads are paved, trams have gone and from the scarred heights dress-circle-homes and sought-after-dwellings stare competitively down on the bay.

Unaware of its value in real estate, as a symbol of status, the bay goes on with its life. Night blots out the suburbs; mists descend; nets of glitter are cast; gulls swoop and come to rest. Beneath a moon full of blood a strange lonely sail flits beside its shadow. In the morning the departing tide leaves the little beach wide and shining. Night dews have smoothed its surface. It lies deserted but for a trotting exploratory dog.

It is still as it was in the days when my whole life focused upon it, when its sounds, colours, moods were part of my growing.

2

Parents

My mother, Florence Amelia Mack, was one of thirteen, the ninth child of a Wesleyan minister and an intellectual matriach. The family grew up in a series of large shabby parsonages, moving every three years according to Methodist custom, by stage coach or steamer or train, around Australia and Tasmania. Since the children were born and educated wherever their father happened to be, my mother was born at Clare, South Australia, and went to school in Sydney.

I have seen some of the houses she lived in, dark, perpendicular, uncompromising, with windows just wide enough to shoot arrows of righteousness from; prim, grim fortresses protecting the godly from a loose sinful world. Even now, painted white, they are chilling; in her youth they must have been doubly daunting in their ugliness, narrowness, height without breadth, set down baldly beside their bleak little mud-coloured churches.

But neither narrow buildings nor narrow religion could crush the Macks' exuberance and vitality. They grew up to live full and colourful lives.

Though such thoughts did not occur to me as a child, I wonder now if my mother was not often lonely, in a particular way. She was busy, of a generation and type that accepted a husband and children as adequate company, though they left her alone all day while they worked or went to school. This was nostalgic loneliness, less a need for present company than a sense of loss for the past; yet there was nothing melancholy in her reminiscences, even when near the end of her life she was the only survivor. To her the past was happiness, fun, companionship of contemporaries and of her sisters. Did she perhaps at the back of her mind feel it all still existed, another suburb of time, to be visited at will if one could arrange to get away, back to the ugly parsonage, the gay brothers and sisters, the stimulating hard-up youth she so clearly remembered, so often described and no doubt secretly longed for?

"I was the *quiet* one," she would say. "The one with no brains."

She said it without apology or resentment, as though brainlessness were a desirable asset. She believed that men preferred women who were not too clever. Had not my father, the most wonderful man in the world, chosen her from among her much cleverer sisters?

Besides, she did not need to be Clever. She was a singer; till she married her life was music, and afterwards music combined with a husband and children. Her beautiful voice was beautifully trained but though she was also an artist, at heart she was always an amateur. She lacked the toughness and drive for battling and being completely *femme d'intérieur* never thought of putting career before marriage. She was a home-maker, the one who listens, looks after, ties up the cuts and brings cups of tea.

Though quiet, she was not really placid. She moved quickly between dramatic despair and gaiety, but in general was irrepressibly optimistic. Everything was always going to turn out all right; things would improve, invalids recover, the highest expectations were entertained, people much better than they appeared, her diamond brooch, lost as regularly as her glasses, would always be found.

To a child she was the voice in the dark after the nightmare, the light shining in from the hall, the sound of singing, the smell of lamb roasting, the background of life.

Having been sat on all her youth by dominant sisters, whom she never ceased to love and admire, my mother compensated by trying to master her children. In this she was defeated by lack of confidence, her own sense of humour and our resilience. Though doting, I do not think she would have got very far with modern Child Experts. Full of complexes herself, she did everything to create them in us—over-protecting Sheila, the first-born, blatantly favouring John, the baby, while I, the middle one, was to be sat on as much as possible.

Sheila, perhaps, suffered most, becoming timid and diffident. John was unspoilable and the more I was slapped down the more I bounced up.

"Go to bed, you're like a little old witch. Hideous!" my mother would say and she told me so often that I was ugly, no doubt to squash vanity, that I believed her.

I cannot remember sobbing my heart out because of it. I knew I had crooked teeth (the supreme misfortune), unlike Sheila's row of pearls, a blob of a nose and a mouth like a shark; but I was so taken up with enjoyment of being alive there was no time to brood. Once, in front of a mirror, cutting my hair, which grew ever shorter as I tried to even it up, I looked at myself in surprise and thought I wasn't really so bad. My eyes and complexion seemed good; but there was no chance to discuss the matter. When my mother saw my Ukrainian peasant hair-cut she cried, "Oh! Your *one* beauty ruined!"

My father, William John Creagh, the youngest of four, grew up in dignified comfort at Elizabeth Bay, in a high Dutch terrace—*Tamworth Mansions*—now facing the dandelion fountain. The Creaghs lived in *The Peel*, the end house with the turret. Across the road, in *Maramanah*, were their life-long friends, the musical Hollanders, now known in local annals as "Aunts up the Cross".

The Creaghs came from Limerick and were soldiers down to the time of my grandfather, who was a lawyer. There was always something rather spare and spartan about them, as though ever ready to strike camp and move off. Law was my father's profession, music and literature his interests, carpentry his hobby, sailing his passion. He had wanted, my mother said, to join the Navy but his father persuaded him it was his duty to do law and take over the practice. The Creaghs were great ones for duty.

Though obliged to console himself with boats smaller than battleships he never ceased hankering for the sea. His obsession took curious forms. My mother claimed he was late for their wedding because he went sailing and got becalmed; and though it was settled that my name was to be Patricia, after my grandfather Patrick, my father, at the last minute, changed it for something more nautical. Sailors' girls were always called Nancy.

Patrick Creagh was a yachtsman and rather a daring one in his time. Eyebrows were raised in the Royal Sydney Yacht Squadron when he came back from Cowes and painted his boat white, all others then being black. He was also one of the first in Sydney to own a centre-board yacht. Since both his sons excelled in sailing it was taken for granted that we, his grandchildren, must also be good in a boat.

At the university my father met my mother's brother, Sidney Mack, a fellow law-student. Taken home to the Parsonage, Billy Creagh found himself in congenial company. In some ways, though not in others, he became more part of my mother's family than his own. It may have been that the Macks just swallowed him up, with their enormous exuberance, or perhaps, my father being not easily swallowed, Mack gaiety and eccentricity appealed to him more than Creagh formality. The Macks called him Billy; to the Creaghs he was Willie.

Compared to the Parsonage, life at *The Peel* must have been dull. People drove in carriages, exchanged calls and left cards. The bright spot was a wild witty cousin, Pierse Shannon, who came out from Ireland for a three-months visit and stayed with the Creaghs thirteen years. He then went back to inherit the family estate and was never heard of again, not even a thank-you letter.

"The Mater loved Pierse," my father would tell us. "He could always get round her. If we got into trouble she would keep it from the Governor, who was rather inclined to be strict, y'know. F'r instance, he wouldn't have cared for us playing the banjo in the streets. . . ."

Willie and Pierse played their banjos outside the pubs in the tougher parts of Kings Cross. They were, they claimed, so good that no one knew they were amateurs. To keep up appearances they accepted money; without compunction from drunks, but not from children. The generosity of the children —poor, ragged, eager to give—eventually drove them out of business but my father remembered those days with great pleasure. So did Mr Justice James, who many years later referred in court to Mr Creagh playing the banjo for money in the streets of Kings Cross.

Though the Creaghs were conventional, Willie was an eccentric at heart. Impatient at times, he was incapable of being bored. Endless vitality, infinite curiosity made each day a new challenge. One of his great pleasures was to take things apart to find out how they worked, though he was less enthusiastic about reassembling them in their original form. Undeterred by possible value, he rode roughshod over rare and beautiful objects that stood in his way. When Nicolette Devas, in *Two Flamboyant Fathers*, says, "a curious trait found in Ireland is the love of fine things with the neglect of fine things, a kind of arrogance that prevents people using a tin-opener rather than the handle of a Georgian silver spoon . . ." she perfectly describes my father. We had not a straight spoon in the house.

There was a strong touch of Japanese in my parents . . . in my mother's submission, her acceptance of lowlier status, her respect, admiration and devotion to her husband, her dedication to her children; and his *samurai* qualities—austerity, frugality, pride, indifference to money, incorruptible loyalty, unimpeachable honour. I think at times she was rather baffled, regarding him as a cross between God and a helpless child. She died believing him the most wonderful of men and never doubted in any way that he was always right, even when, in the days of their courtship, he drove her up Oxford Street at peak hour on the wrong side of the road. The nearest to criticism I ever heard, when he polished his shoes on a clean towel or left his clothes on the floor was, "Spoilt! Brought up in a houseful of servants!"

Yet in many ways he was extremely easy-going, even detached; so detached he omitted to register my birth, which has not yet been recorded. He had his own world of law, friends, sailing, music, books. His life and ours overlapped in the last three and for the rest he left us more or less to our mother. I doubt if he knew that she used him at times as a threat: "You wait till Dad hears. . . ." "If your father *knew*. . . ."

If, occasionally, he did punish us, it was with the attitude of a researcher trying a new technique; as when John, having shared his father's best cigars with friends, was made, green-faced and sweating, to smoke another.

Apart from their children, my parents' great bond was music. I cannot remember a time in our house without it, from the moment we got up till late at night. We went to the piano each morning as regularly as to the shower; we returned to it after school. During the day my mother played and sang for herself. At odd moments she would fling down what she was doing and dash to the drawingroom for a couple of hours. Coming home from school you heard her singing as you entered the gate, and went, bread and honey in hand, to lean and listen or be given a lesson; for as our father expected us to be good in a boat, she expected us all to sing.

At night my father played records and we neglected our homework to listen, on the moonlit veranda, by the dining-room fire, upstairs in our bedrooms. At all hours he was to be found lying back in his chair, cap over eyes, John's one-eyed cat on his chest, absorbed in Bach, Purcell, Vivaldi, Handel, Haydn, Mozart, Gluck, Beethoven or Schubert. He claimed that nothing had been written since Schubert. The exception was Sullivan's music, which, allied to Gilbert's wit, was a constant part of our lives.

After the evening music, with cigars or a pipe, he would sleep in his armchair, waking about midnight to make tea and start the night's reading. This went on till two or three o'clock. He then slept till seven, got up, had breakfast and took the eight-fifteen tram into town.

Leaving his office in the evening he would walk briskly down to the Quay, stopping at Tyrell's Bookshop, at Nock and Kirby's for a few nails and screws, or mechanical toys for us—later he went to Woolworths, for his grandchildren— then on, swinging the cane he always carried, to the ferry he always caught and his accustomed seat on the outside deck. Here he would resume his reading, from time to time rousing himself to cast a watchful eye on the life of the harbour.

Though in old age deafness deprived him of music, the reading continued; nor did the weight or quality of the books diminish—history, politics, economics, current affairs, the English classics, philosophy and the Latin poets in the original.

Books were an integral part of his life, whatever the crisis. After my mother's funeral he was found immersed in the *Trial and Death of Socrates*; and when, at the age of ninety, he was badly hurt in a road accident, he did not lose his head. Prone, covered with blood, in the casualty ward, he issued instructions.

"I shall require a few essentials brought round, if you please, as soon as possible. Bring my toothbrush, my Horace, my Shakespeare."

3

Jemima

Since my mother had twelve brothers and sisters and most of them had reproduced, we had any amount of cousins, as well as uncles and aunts. Yet though so well off for other relations we lacked grandfathers. It was not till I went to kindergarten that I learnt these were almost as common as grandmothers and that well-equipped children had two of each. Even then I felt no deprivation. Unfamiliar with ageing men, uncorrupted by pity or understanding I recoiled from the grandpas of my friends, grey-faced dotards in cardigans, sitting about all day, dribbling and dropping food, shuffling in slippers, speaking in high thin voices. I sensed and hated the inner softness, the sexlessness of these unthroned males.

Our own departed grandfathers, photographed in their prime, retained their good looks and manly vigour: Patrick William Creagh, stern, aristocratic, dignified, with grey imperial and light eyes that suggested a twinkle; Hans Mack, luscious with shiny black beard, fine dark eyes, romantic, soft, rather sexy.

Hans was born in County Down in 1831 and brought to Australia by the Methodist church in 1854, with fifteen other young Irish ministers. A few—Kelynack, Windeyer, Carruthers—remained family friends into later generations.

In Kiama, on the South Coast, where Hans was sent, he

met a sprightly young woman from Armagh, named Jemima James. He gave her a Bible, inscribed with the point of a pin in brown ink, in characters gothic as Chartres cathedral, and married her when she was eighteen. Jemima's father was rich, Hans was poor; but poverty did not disconcert her. By the time she was thirty-five she had thirteen children.

Hans died at the age of fifty-eight, on his way back from Europe, long before my parents were married. He is a stranger to me, apart from snippets heard from his daughters, and a curious description in *The History of Methodism in Australia*:

> In temperament he was warm and impulsive, but a true and generous friend. As a Pastor, he was sympathetic and tender, as a student diligent, and as a Preacher, he gave evidence of a penetrating mind, while his sermons were marked by solidity and weight.

From my mother and aunts I learnt only that he was very strict, that he bought in bulk at sales for economy and the family had to wear or eat his purchases, so that feet and digestions were ruined early in life. A bigoted puritan, despite—or perhaps because of—his luscious good looks, he abstained from all pleasures except those domestic activities sanctioned as Duty by Wesley, St Paul and Queen Victoria.

The dominant figure remains Jemima, trailing round Australia after Hans with her expanding family, a book eternally in her hand, educating her children, reading late into the night, mending and making clothes, battling with cheap half-wit servants on the South Coast, the North Coast, in South Australia and Tasmania, at Braidwood during the Gold Rush, at Windsor on the Hawkesbury, in the Sydney slums of Newtown and Redfern. Though always hard-up, her children had the best possible education, having first learnt to read from their mother. Pointing out the words with a knitting needle, she took them through whatever book she was reading at the time. My mother, whose lessons coincided with *Macaulay's Essays*, thus learnt at the age of five that Bacon died of a chill caught while stuffing a fowl in the snow.

Perhaps Jemima's father helped educate the boys, for few of them went to church schools where they might have had concessions. The two eldest were at the Methodist Prince Alfred College in Adelaide, where the second son, Hans, as we were so often told, was School Captain at the age of fourteen. He was also one of the first three graduates of Adelaide University and took his Arts degree at eighteen, before going to England to study medicine.

Jemima was pioneer material, strong, autocratic, valiant, resourceful. When her husband died she struggled on alone, refusing to let her sons leave the university to take jobs, keeping the younger children at school till the family were educated, married or given professions.

After that, for a short time, she was free to submerge herself in her books; then her sight failed. Friends said how ironic, how cruel that she of all people should go blind; but the family knew she was paying for the long hours of sewing and reading by candlelight during their childhood.

Jemima herself, without complaint or self-pity, briskly adapted to her changed condition. By the time we knew her she was quite blind; yet never was anyone less like a poor blind grandmother, nor visiting antique relations less of a chore. Not that she was at all cosy, in fact she was rather formidable; but time spent with her was never long enough.

Still directing the lives of her middle-aged married children, she lived with our youngest aunt in a house higher up on our hill. Reduced gentlewomen came and went as Companions, worn to shreds by endless reading aloud, crushed by tart comments on faulty pronunciation or gaps in literary knowledge.

Jemima was fey. She had second-sight, though she could not be persuaded to talk of it and even disapproved of her gift. "Stuff and nonsense!" she would say when such incidents were mentioned.

But the power could not be denied, least of all on her deathbed. Too weak to move, she had drifted into unconsciousness and remained thus for days. Then, to her daughters' astonishment she sat up, as though seeing someone, called "*Hans!*" and immediately died.

"Strange!" said my mother and aunts, cabling the news to the family in England. "After all these years, our father's name on her lips as she died!"

The cable crossed with a letter coming from London. Our Uncle Hans, the son Jemima had not seen for forty years, was dead. They had both died the same day, and as he died he had roused himself and called "Mother!"

From the balcony where Jemima sat facing the ocean she could not see, the scenery fell into perspective. Grotto Point and the tide-marking headland appeared closer, the bay itself somehow smaller, more enclosed, the open stretch towards the Heads wider, more spread out. You could see the rocks at the base of North Head where the water broke and swirled and retreated or on blue days lay calm and relaxed into silk. The high cliff no longer seemed a familiar harbour boundary but coastal, part of the open seas that stretched away to foreign lands, Greece, Italy, the shores of Japan. From our house, its sharp toothless-Red-Indian profile was uncomplex and two-dimensional; from this greater height, when light struck down obliquely through powdery triangles of mist and fine spray, recesses were thrown into relief and the cliff-face became a ruined amphitheatre sloping towards the sea.

On hassocks, hugging our knees, we sat at the feet of our grandmother, listening intently to her stupendous world of history, literature, personal reminiscence, the Old and New Testament. Her telling was hypnotic, explicit, heavily partisan, so superbly detailed that one always knew how people looked and spoke, what they ate and wore. It was said that the Creagh children talked of Abraham and Isaac and the Kings of England as though they lived next door. Day after day through our childhood we sat, spellbound to silence, while below, Tyrrhenian-tranquil, the ocean basked and slumbered against piled rocks and weightless ships glided trackless over its surface, suspended from columns of smoke.

"How do you ride side-saddle, Nan Mack? How do you stay on?"

"It is very comfortable and far more becoming than riding like *men*. You wear a beautiful habit and there is a horn on the saddle for you to put your knee round. . . ."

Dark eyes shining, thick silver hair brushed back high like a marquise from her handsome forehead, she was absorbed in her tale, while we examined her strange elastic-sided boots, her gold-topped cane, the Victorian brooch at her throat which, spookily, might contain a lock of Hans's dead hair. From this angle she was majestic, imperious; never did I sense despair or self-pity; yet sometimes . . .

"Help me inside!" she would order, standing up, holding her cane, and walking behind, my hand on her back, there came a disturbing sensation. The strong face, the valiant eyes were the marquise; the back was a frail old woman feeling her way in the dark. Confused, embarrassed, with tears in my throat, I wished to escape. Security, all life were threatened. Only her sharp commands to her downtrodden Companion could restore my sense of normality.

Jemima's hands were thin, with long fingers and transparent skin. White, fine, cared-for, they lay on her lap, holding a handkerchief scented with lavender-water, their work done.

"I'll finish the story tomorrow. Off you go, your mother will be worrying. And be careful crossing the road."

A kiss on the soft cheek, a breath of lavender-water, a touch of the delicate claw, of bird-bones in a silky sheath; then a wild scamper down the Quarry Steps, back to our kingdom.

At Jemima's there was a drawingroom with deep blue carpet and books and piano; in the bathroom, oval violet-scented Roger and Gallet soap; in the diningroom, black horse-hair chairs you stuck to in summer, and port-wine jelly and egg-custard made with a bay leaf, served in little glasses with handles.

Jemima rarely went out except to visit her old school friend, Amelia Pemmel. Miss Pemmel was a stout black presence faintly smelling of perspiration, with 18th-century gunmetal glasses and tusk-like hairs sprouting from enlarged pores. She was probably very godly. She lived with a pug lap-dog in a dark high narrow Methodist house, as intimidating as her black clothes and gold chains and elastic-sided boots. I value her now as a period piece, as a visible link briefly joining me to a past age; but in those days I shrank from the coarse face and spiky whiskers I had to kiss, the perspiring black smell.

While she and Jemima discoursed, addressing each other as Mrs Mack and Miss Pemmel, I was left to amuse myself with the pug; but it was so old, so bad-tempered, so sniffly and slobbery and stuffed-up in the head that I feared to touch it. It smelt of very old dog and was going bald here and there.

Jemima, being blind, did not mind sitting in the dark, and my aunt, having brought us here, had gone out to do shopping. I was trapped till her return in this sombre room with a wheezing old dog and two pairs of elastic-sided boots, for as usual I sat on a hassock; yet I was fascinated. Was it the contrast, the interior gloom and the dry hot westerly blowing outside; the old ladies' subdued gentle voices conversing so formally, so strangely unlike the way other people talked? Or the sense of being in a capsule shut off from time, a world of red Turkey carpets and chamber-pots, of mahogany sideboards and port wine for invalids? The outer air, the sun never entered this room; the bay and the beach might not exist. The whole house was sealed. If you strayed into the narrow hall with its stairs, vertical as an empty bookcase (*What was upstairs?*) you felt the silence ring in your ears, static, preserved, lifeless, *embalmed*.

Jemima's beautiful hands had worked hard; the little hands of Louisa, our grandmother Creagh, which had never done anything rougher than embroidery, were knotted and twisted with rheumatism. We did not notice their ugliness, seeing only her vivid blue eyes, silky complexion and beautiful white wavy hair. We called her Nan Tay. Doll-sized, irresponsible, sparkling with mischief and wit, she wore bonnets which she called her *corbeen*, with feathers, jet beads and wide ribbons tied under the chin, and spoke with a soft brogue, no more than the trace of a lisp. Her conversation was full of Irish words and expressions for though she was brought to Australia in infancy, her Irish nurse Brigit remained with her till she married.

She was sixteen when she married Patrick William, whom she always addressed and referred to as Mr Creagh, even when speaking to us. Though I never saw him—he died the week I was born—I felt she was in awe, not only of him but of her children, except perhaps my father, the youngest and gayest.

From Brigit she had also acquired a strange confusion of stories of Ireland and Irish sufferings, of wakes, dispossessed tenants, starving peasants and bogs. Her sense of history was weak and the persecutions of Queen Elizabeth, Cromwell and Queen Victoria were all one. We learnt a great deal about peasants, that they burnt earth instead of wood or coal, that they hung a dried herring from the ceiling and pointed their boiled potato at it as they ate—a meal called Potato and Point; that landlords were monsters, the English were devils, that pigs lived under the bed and were known as The Gentleman who Pays the Rent. My two Creagh aunts, who did not much care for these tales, pointed out that their mother could not have seen much of peasant life. Not only did she leave Ireland as a baby, her father was a solicitor living in Dublin; but when they reminded us that Ireland was not just a bog full of peasants and pigs, that there were also Irish gentry to which the Creaghs belonged, Louisa took it as a personal insult and talked sarcastically about snobs and aristocrats.

Unlike the Macks, there were not many Creagh relations ... two Mackerras cousins, Louisa's elder sister *Poor Mairyan*, a stout petrified old lady who lived in a nursing-home, and three wonderful shadows called Tomasina, Phoebe and Grace, in a dim house at Mosman Bay. Charming, sweet, gracious, with very soft hands and murmuring voices they smelt of lavender-water and fed us with cakes and sweets. They were attended by the first Aboriginal I ever saw, a gentle motherly creature called Lizzie, adopted in infancy by Aunt Tomasina when she lived on the Manning River.

These were courtesy step-great-aunts of some complex kind. My great-grandfather, Jasper Creagh, from Limerick, having left the Army and been widowed in Antigua, brought his four children to Australia, where he married an Irish widow with seven of her own. Of his first wife's family, one was my grandfather Patrick; another was Albert, who, my Creagh aunts liked to tell us, *married his sister, Tomasina*! Then, while we goggled, they would explain that whereas Tomasina's father was the late Mr Maunsell, Albert's mother had been the late Mary Auchinleck.

I have often wondered how the skittish rebellious young Louisa fitted into my dignified grandfather's life. Her tongue was far from discreet, her aversions strong and irrational. They included Catholics, doctors, all kinds of clergy and Men Who Smell their Hats in Church (in the days when men stood holding their hats to their bosoms). Though Southern Irish and quite irreligious, she was full of perverse Protestant prejudice. In the past, the Creaghs were Catholics (and still are in Ireland), who suffered persecution and imprisonment for their faith. Richard Creagh, a 16th-century scholar, Bishop of Armagh, Primate of Ireland, was twice imprisoned in the Tower, from which he once escaped and in which he finally died. (I cannot read his works; they are in Latin.) My grandfather's sister Elizabeth, educated in Paris by the Sacré Coeur, became a nun; but we were not Catholics for Patrick backslid. I do not know how Louisa felt when at his death his sister produced a priest. He lies in the Catholic section of Waverley Cemetery.

It was not really inconsistent that though fulminating against Catholics in general, Louisa loved her nun sister-in-law. Her anti-Catholicism was mainly a pose and at heart I doubt if she cared either way. When Catholic priests called, she said she was Presbyterian; when Protestant parsons came she said she was Catholic.

Days at Louisa's were quite unlike those at Jemima's. The Creagh house was well-kept, polished and cold, the furniture more expensive and uglier, the view out through the Heads grander but less intimate and poetic. My two aunts, single and widowed, kept to their rooms, doing exquisite embroidery, making spider-web lace. When Nan Tay's hands grew too crippled for such work she tatted beautiful borders and medallions to be set into tea-cloths and table-centres for my mother, whom she adored. She would tell us that our grandfather taught her to tat with rope, out in the boat.

Before and after lunch you sat in her room with your back to the view, eating humbugs, listening to her low lisping persuasive voice recounting stories of Ireland, restively learning to sew, knit, tat, crochet, embroider, do drawn-thread and Venetian work. The Creagh women took it for granted that Sheila and I must have these accomplishments, and we were each given sets of the best equipment for practising them. Jemima and my mother felt such elegant pursuits a waste of time, a mere incentive to gossip.

Even when not eating humbugs, Louisa's jaws gently munched up and down in a way we found endearing and funny. From time to time she would murmur, "I wonder what o'clock it is?" and dip down into her small plumped-up bosom and fish out a beautiful little watch in Limoges enamel. "Blow on it!" she would say as she pressed the catch, so the front seemed to open at one's breath; then she would inspect the dial, press a little knob to make it chime sweetly, hold it against one's ear, close and return the watch down her front saying, " 'Twas my sainted mother's, and when I'm gone 'twill be Sheila's."

Meals at Nan Tay's were good but rather formal and starched—starched napkins, starched cloth, starched conversation. Only the housekeeper, a licensed Malaprop, chattered at table. When my Uncle Albert was down from Tamworth, where he was the other half of Creagh & Creagh, Solicitors, the silence was almost complete. He was not really formidable, though inclined to sarcasm, but his mother and sisters had built an aura of such divinity round him one was afraid to utter a sound. So strangely divine was he that we were not even allowed to go anywhere near the bathroom in case he see us, or we him, coming or going to the lavatory (known as The Place). If you needed to use it, watches were posted to see where Y'r'uncle was, then the signal given to make a dash.

Victorian prudishness was not native to Louisa; at heart she was rather saucy, her wit inclined to be risqué. Spontaneous wit such as hers disappoints in re-telling; it needs the significant glance, the droll inflection, the speed with which it shoots out, like a snake's tongue, to deflate pomposity, pretention, stupidity.

Bishops were her favorite targets, the more stately and unctuous the better.

"Ah, my dear Mrs Creagh," a well-known cleric intoned, bending over her chair. "And are you going to give me some of your beautiful embroidery for our Sale of Work?"

"Indeed no," Louisa said mildly. "But I'll give you something much better."

"And what is that, dear lady?" the Bishop asked, washing his hands in the air.

"A jolly good tip for the Melbourne Cup!"

The Bishop recoiled.

"I wouldn't touch the devil's money!" he said sternly.

"Faith, I wouldn't trust you with it."

"Madam," the Bishop warned. "You go too far! You should keep a guard on your lips!"

"What kind, my lord?" Louisa said, raising her cornflower eyes. "A tram-guard?"

4

A Flight of Parakeets

THE Macks were impassioned throwers-out but the Creaghs were hoarders. Even during my childhood our attics were filling up fast with junk that might come in and objects that clearly could never come in but could not be parted with. As time passed and relations died, went abroad or moved into smaller houses the accumulation increased till eventually all five attics, the disused cellar-laundry, the vast area under the house were full.

As well as her fruitless fight against hoarding my mother had to contend with our untidiness. Ours was the sort of house where door hinges were used as nutcrackers; and books, papers and alien objects crowded under beds and on tops of wardrobes. My father, who meticulously rolled up string and kept nails graded in special boxes, threw most of his clothes on the floor, while we children regarded our large separate bed-rooms as licence to live each in our own individual state of disorder.

Domestic life was further complicated by animals—birds, white mice, guinea-pigs, goldfish, tadpoles, lugubrious spaniels, humourless Alsatians, eager fox-terriers, maudlin stray mongrels called Towser, fecund cats, endless kittens, and possums. Against my mother's strictest orders the dogs and cats were fed in the house, sometimes at table, and slept on our beds.

Possums, normally fed outside, often wandered indoors, clumped upstairs, tugged at table-cloths, upset china or leapt in blind panic upon polished furniture which they scarified with their claws. Cats gave birth in hat-boxes, Budgerigars, escaped from cages, flew into puddings or up into shelves of plates; tortoises lay submerged in bath or wash-basin. Forgotten tadpoles, perishing of neglect, stank in congealing jam-jars under beds.

The possums lived in the roof. They made marks on the ceilings and at night thumped, rattled, hissed, fought, gave hair-raising throttled groans and screams as they pounded lustfully after each other over rafters and up lath-and-plaster walls. My mother complained; nervous visitors had cold sweats, no one could sleep, but we never considered getting rid of these favoured pests. Trained by my father, tame as cats, they had been pensioners for years. Each new generation, brought in infancy by their mothers to eat bread-and-milk, came with their own young. The mothers would sit on their haunches, holding the bread in their delicate claws while beady black eyes sparkled out from their pouches. As the infants grew stronger the females came more clumsily, thumping down heavily with babies clinging desperately to their backs. As they ate, bare trembling pink noses, sets of quivering whiskers and boot-button eyes could be glimpsed between the mother's ears or over their shoulders.

So timid yet brave, so tame yet so wild, they came at my whistle and sat while I stroked them, yet at the slightest alarm would bound away into the trees, baby on back. Understanding their need for a quick get-away, my father constructed a series of spring-boards round the back veranda. The possums always used them for taking-off, unlike our cats and dogs who ignored the special flaps and entrances he had cut for them in fences and gates.

Our garden was large, full of exotic shrubs and sheltered corners. A winding secluded path and steps led from the kitchen door, under cactus and palm, to the back gate—known as the

Tradesmen's Entrance—on Parrawi Road. By the front gate were the cypress-trees that gave their name to our street. Years later—the first slow crack in the porcelain of permanence—the garden was sliced in half to make room for a new road to Chinaman's Beach, and the beautiful cypresses fell, taking our childhood world with them.

At the back, the garden sloped to a bushland gully, where fern-filled caves were moist on the hottest days and thick native trees and plants grew wild. Convolvulus and lantana threatened cultivated hibiscus and poinsettia, nasturtiums lay orange and red underfoot. A winding path, a little bridge over a stream led to the wooden garage, high on stilts like Baba Yaga's house, entered from the back by steep steps and a cobwebby door. Here, white ants lived happily, eating away undisturbed for generations until the night when the last bite was taken. The garage then collapsed, never to rise again.

In this moist ferny gully I learnt, among other things, to climb perilous trees, drink water from moss, do the drawback and chew tobacco. My companions were John and his friends, little boys summoned from neighboring hills by the yodelling-wardling cry known to children all over the world. My mother complained that I was a tomboy. She also warned of snakes, and ticks which fastened into our scalps and had to be got out with kerosene.

Each year these ticks killed our pets by slow paralysis; each year the long-drawn-out agony of doomed cats or dogs broke our hearts. Each year, burying them with elaborate rites in the garden, we swore with sobs to have no more animals; each year we succumbed again to hapless strays or welcomed with ecstatic screams small furry objects produced, warm and squirming, from my father's pocket.

No matter how early, there was always a fishing boat on the bay, small, anonymous, bone-shaped, low in the water, dark against the glitter. Sometimes a solitary man bent over the line, sometimes two made the eternal symbol of patience.

On warm grey evenings nets were drawn in to the little beach. Seagulls circled, dogs and children ran. The dogs waded recklessly into the water and stood, paw raised, barking hysterically, swivelling uneasy eyes at threshing fish; the children shrieked as young sharks or monstrous rays were heaved from the net.

At night soft putterings rose from Italian prawning boats. In the moonless dark little flickering yellow lamps crossed the bay. Familiar, the background of daily life, it was timeless and universal and ever-new.

From time to time our quiet kingdom by the sea was shot through with colour and movement. Like flights of parakeets, Mack relations who had gone abroad before our birth or during our infancy began coming home to roost. Disembodied names with geographical labels—Aunty Louie in Italy, Uncle Launce in Mesopotamia, Aunty Amy in England, Aunty Alice in India, Uncle Gus in Russia, the little Macks in London, the little Macks in Japan—appeared in the flesh. New cousins arrived, pale fair Harry-san from Kobe, to board at Shore, Mary Hamilton Mack from London, a Slade student whose paintings in the Augustus John manner were considered Most Extraordinary.

There were tearful reunions, marvelling exclamations, dinner parties. Flats were taken, houses searched for, bought and moved into. My mother simmered all day with excitement. Never since childhood, never again did she have so many of her family at hand, safe and well.

Until the parakeets began to homeward fly we knew only one Mack aunt—Gertrude, the youngest, whom we called Dimsie. She was a pianist. At an early age, claiming I was unmanageable and my hair straggly, my mother sent me to live with her for six months. When I returned I had thick lustrous wavy hair and a new personality. Of the hair, Dimsie said, "I cut a fringe and the rest went wavy." Of the changed demeanour, which did not last, "She only wants to be treated as a reasonable being. She'll do anything if you tell her WHY."

Since my mother's answer to WHY? was "Because I tell you to, Miss!" Dimsie's astonishing attitude convinced me she was my true mother, that I had been adopted by my official parents because she had no husband. Sometimes, awarding my parentage to those I loved best, I thought I might be the child of my father and Dimsie, or of Dimsie and a favorite uncle. Though I loved my mother I had to share her with Sheila and John. With Dimsie I was the only one.

She was pretty, slim, elegant, clever. She cooked beautiful food, wore ravishing clothes (flowered chiffons, cloche hats, red velvet opera cloaks with pink georgette lining), had exquisite underwear, heavenly scents. Her pillow-cases were embroidered, her nightgowns threaded with blue satin ribbon. She allowed me to paw through her wardrobe, her chest of drawers, to daub my face with her powder, soak in her bath-salts. At home there was always music but Dimsie played for me alone, so I thought, crouched on the floor beneath the piano watching her feet on the pedals, or lying in bed, in a new lacy nightgown, sobbing without knowing why, at the *Waldstein*.

Though she looked like a flower, she had her mother's courage and strength. Jemima had adapted, without complaint, to blindness. Dimsie, whose whole life had been music, made a new career as a journalist when cancer surgery took her music away.

Dimsie travelled a great deal and the presents she brought back were always exciting—clay Mexican animals, bright wooden Russian dolls, sad gentle Japanese folk-toys wrapped in fine scented paper, fragile underwear or exotic pyjamas.

She also brought fresh admirers, to add to the permanent retinue of faithful followers we accepted as Family. The newcomers were usually Intellectuals and to our minds food for mockery. Hawk-eyed, Sheila and I would watch each betraying detail, scenting out any faint aberration or trace of femininity; then, the visitor gone, commence our heartless impersonations. The cultured tones of these intellectuals—frequently maiden

29

gentlemen—their urgent, emphatic, so-called Oxford accents made them easy to mimic. They spat when they talked or had cotton reels in their mouths.

They were all victimized—eminent academics, scientists, writers, doctors and diplomats, the more distinguished the better.

"Little *savages!*" Dimsie would expostulate. "If you could only hear your own ghastly voices, your frightful Osstrylian accents. Your *kyke* and *plyce* and *keow* and *heowse*. You're just like your mother! How anyone ever got husbands with her in the house!"

And my mother would giggle as though paid a great compliment.

Suddenly, there were more aunts, two of whom wrote books, the bird-loving Amy Eleanor, the intrepid Marie Louise. Louise, who went to London before I was born, was a legend, mysterious, wonderful, daring. She was an Authoress. She wrote her first book when she was seventeen; she was the author of *Teens* and *Girls Together*, still widely read in those days, and countless grown-up novels. She was photographed wrapped in sables, had a flat in the Adelphi, a villa in Italy. She was said to be beautiful, fascinating, terribly brave, and had outwitted the whole German army in occupied Antwerp during The War, where she went as a war correspondent. I never expected to see her, would not have believed she existed had she not once flashed briefly and terribly across my infant sky.

Three years old, in red shoes and white organdie embroidered with little Dutch girls, I was sat on the grass and told to wait, to be good and not eat clay, for Aunty Louie was taking us all to the pantomime. When my mother came out with John in her arms and Sheila in white muslin with blue shoes I was still sitting, legs outstretched and apart as though starched, afraid to move lest I lose this mysterious treat.

The abstraction I had heard called Aunty Louie was a luxurious scent, a swirl of plumes, a gleam of lilac satin, a squeeze of white kid gloves, a gay chuckling voice and a wonderful approving warmth. In a Box—she never took less—our mouths stuffed with rich chocolates, we sat, stupefied with excitement at our first taste of theatre.

I stared, incredulous, at this exotic world of colour and fantasy, so much more real than the world we had left outside. I wanted it never to end, to be in it myself, be part of it, never to go home again; but the scene changed. Slave girls, eunuchs were gone. Alone, in a greenish light, Bluebeard's last wife opened a door and revealed the heads of the other wives hanging over a red-splashed wall.

Though not understanding, I grew uneasy. Then the lights went out on a ballet in black tights with white phosphorescent bones and skulls. I began to cry. Terrified, beating off my mother's assurance that they were only pussy-cats, I sobbed to go home.

It was not only the skeletons. When the lights came on, the warm smiling silken aunt had changed. Regarding me acidly, she made cutting remarks about Cowards and Cry Babies and what the little Belgian children endured in the bombardment of Antwerp, not to mention the little Mack cousins in London with the Zeppelins. I cried more than ever and had to be taken out in disgrace, for John, too young to understand why, was now crying in sympathy.

"Just like Lou," my mother said to my father. "You never know where you are with her."

He grunted and asked what she expected. He found Louise at this time exceedingly trying, living grandly at The Australia, whirling round the country lecturing for the Red Cross on her war experiences, autographing her books.

To me she had become a nightmare threat with her icy sarcasm and contempt; but soon she vanished without a word and was not seen again for twelve years. This, the family said, was typical.

Though Louise was frightening she had a glamour no other relation possessed. Her younger sister, who wrote as Amy Eleanor Mack and whose books were known and loved by all our contemporaries, could never compete in our minds, for all our affection. She was a stranger when she came back into our lives, several years after Louise disappeared, and though she had dedicated *Scribbling Sue* to us we knew little about her. Our mother's tales of her adult life abroad lacked the drama of Louie's adventures. We knew vaguely that Amy wrote, that she had married the Love of her Life, Launcelot Harrison, who was handsome and brilliant and with whom she went to Cambridge. Then the war came and he went to Mesopotamia while she stayed in London with the Zeppelins.

Now, my mother told us, our Aunt Amy and Uncle Launce were coming home. They had already left London and in six weeks the Orient Liner would steam through the Heads and we would see them. The ship was at Aden, then Colombo. Soon it was next week, then tomorrow, then today and we were up at sunrise, staring out from the balcony at the high black ship entering the Heads.

After breakfast we were taken, beside ourselves with excitement, to Jemima's, where we found her, in black crepe-de-chine with lace bertha and sardonyx brooch, sitting in state in the drawingroom. This was strange, at half-past eight in the morning; strange too, to find the hall full of uncles and aunts and older cousins. Tea was being made in the kitchen and scones and sandwiches put out on silver dishes. Though thrilling, it was confusing and rather unnerving. Even our dear Dimsie seemed too busy to talk to us. John and I slunk away into a corner. No one missed us. Our mother seemed to have forgotten us. She and Sheila were in the drawingroom with the grown-ups.

A tall man, a small woman came up the steps to the house. There was laughter, kissing and hugging. My mother cried and everyone talked at once. The tall man picked me up in his arms. I struggled and cried to be set down. John and I clung together. People laughed and bent over us, faces came close, encouraging noises were made but we shrank back and presently were alone. They had all gone into the drawingroom and the door was shut.

This was not at all what we had expected, much less wanted. It was bad enough to be rushed but worse to be excluded. Anti-climax set in; we felt neglected, ill-used at being taken so literally. It was the piercing disappointment of not being pressed to the coveted slice of cake refused for good manners.

What had gone wrong? Dimly we felt it had all happened too quickly. Legendary figures, so familiar, safe and desirable in the distance, had too suddenly come too close. In the flesh they were too overpowering and strange to be accepted at once. We needed time, and this the grown-ups should have known or understood. They should have insisted, persuading us gently but they were all too excited to care.

In the hall, on the balcony, luggage was piled, smelling of leather and canvas—suitcases, trunks, all kinds of boxes and crates, and bundles of carpets with fringes, wrapped round walking sticks and long-handled tropical umbrellas. The smells were new and strange, not like the smells at home, not even like those at our Aunt Alice's house—the scents of Japan and China, of Indian sandalwood and Burmese incense. This was a different foreignness. It hinted at ravishing presents, exotic surprises, an unknown and marvellous world.

But no one came to unpack the boxes, to unwrap the Persian rugs. We grew disconsolate. If only They would open the door and beg us to come in. Pride would not let us enter, though we tried to attract attention by gently kicking the panels. We were not noticed, nor heard above the chatter. We were going to be left out for ever.

Bored, restless, we began to sing. Uncle Launce was a soldier. We would sing him a recruiting song learnt at kindergarten. Marching up and down the hall we chirrupped hopefully:

"Soldier Boy, Soldier Boy, whairhair are you go-wing?
Bearing so proudly your red, white and blue?"

"I'm go-wing to fight for my Ki-hi-hing and Country
If you-hoo'll be a Soldier Boy you can come too."

When you sang the song at school you had a Union Jack
and you stopped in front of someone and offered the flag.
They took it and fell in behind until at last there was a long
line; but with only two of us it wasn't much fun. And though
we marched and stamped and sang louder, each time coming
closer to the door, They still didn't hear.

At last we sank down in discouragement, singing mournfully
to ourselves:

> *Now my dears you must know,*
> *It's a long time ago,*
> *There were two little children*
> *Whose names I don't know.*
>
> *They wandered away*
> *On a bright sunny day,*
> *And were lost in the wild woods,*
> *So I've heard people say . . . .*

Overcome with the pathos of our position our voices were
plaintive, close to tears. Suddenly the door opened. Recognized,
rescued, dragged in, we were kissed, hugged and handed round
in a glow of remorseful tenderness. At once shyness was gone.

Sitting on Uncle Launce's knee I could see large blue eyes
in a handsome brown face. He wore a tweed jacket with buttons of plaited leather and smelt of leather, tobacco and shaving
soap. He laughed. He was the handsomest man I had ever
seen and unmistakably male. I fell madly in love.

Amy was small, warm and brown, like a bird or little fur
animal. She smoked incessantly and her laughs ended in rack-

ing coughs. We had never before seen a woman smoke but my mother was too happy to disapprove. We sensed at once that this uncle and aunt were different, would always be on our side, that they knew about children as clearly as though they had never forgotten their own childhood. They were fellow-conspirators rather than Grown-ups. Amy was even close to us in size. It was she who had heard our sad song outside when all the others were deaf.

Sheila, two years older than I, was already enslaved; even John, eighteen months younger, could not resist. When Uncle Launce bent down and asked, "How old are you, Johnny Creagh?" John said gruffly but fearlessly, "I'm free'n'arf"; and unperturbed by the laughter, his blue eyes looked trustingly into Launce's blue eyes, friend meeting friend.

5

It was the Music

MY mother was the only one of the five Mack girls who did not attempt to write. She would never have dared, it was not her function; yet she had the eye, tongue and selective memory of a writer. Since she also acted and mimicked with innocent malice we felt we had shared most of her youth.

The sisters look out from their girlish photographs—my mother, Florence Amelia, under black velvet picture hat with enormous plumes; Amy Eleanor, in off-the-shoulder tulle, languishing, signed *Toujours à toi*; Alice Emily, head slightly lowered so her immense brown eyes seem to gaze sentimentally up into yours; Marie Louise, eyes cast down, in a large straw hat tied with a chiffon scarf under the chin; Gertrude, in white with an 18-inch waist, fresh and exquisitely virginal. In their pin-tucked lawns and muslins and *broderie anglais* you would say butter would not melt in their mouths.

You would be wrong, even with my mother, so lamblike, silent and shy. Though she sat in the background, blushing when spoken to, she missed no tiny physical or social absurdity. When her sisters' beaux had departed she would gently apply the pinprick that deflated romantic illusions and sowed dissatisfaction.

"He's quite handsome but for his nose. . . ." "He turns his toes out . . . ." "He crooks his little finger . . . ." "He says, 'In a manner of speaking' . . . ."

Such comments were made without spite or envy, in the pure detachment of the artist. All the sisters shared an intense interest in and love of people as types, a relish for oddities, a merciless eye. There was also a talent for extracting ridiculous essentials, to be wickedly described in a family shorthand made up of inflections, glances and key words.

One of these key words is *Bod*, indispensible to initiates, meaningless to others. It is also a yardstick, since the world consists of those who understand it and those who don't. Explanations are useless. It is an Irish flash, a word from the side of the mouth, a nudge of the elbow.

My mother, obligingly trying to explain to our school friends, fumbled with definitions: "A Bod is someone who wears elastic-sided boots in their mind. Homely; a nice cup of tea; Don't Mind If I Do; Bod feet; a Bod hat, brown felt, perched, turned up at the back. Never nasty; rather dowdy; amiable, kind; young men singing tenor solos in drawingrooms; 'O Promise Me' at weddings; potted palms; toes turned out; 'As the saying is'; but *all in the mind*."

Those who understood, used the word correctly at once; others grasped only its literal sense, were bewildered to hear the Duchess of York described as an Absolute Bod.

"But it's nothing to do with position or money," my mother tried to clarify. "It's in the mind. It's a kind of *person*." Then, increasing confusion, "Person's a Bod word. 'A Lovely Person' is terribly Bod. But it's not only people or even words. There are Bod houses, furniture, music, meals . . . anything."

I do not think she was ever bored, however depressed, fed-up or frustrated. She was a transmuter of life, one of those who take in, transform and reissue as art or in personal contact, whose source never dries up. We never tired of hearing about her youth, her sisters, her days as a music student. The people of these adventures were so vivid, so mixed in my mind I accepted them all, even characters from Italian opera, as part of our family.

Signor Steffani, her singing master, and his wife were dead

long before we were born but we knew every detail of their house on Pittwater—just like the Italian lakes—where they entertained their favorite pupils, talking Italian, singing Italian, eating Italian food. We knew that Italian opera was the only opera, apart from Mozart; Italy the most beautiful country, Italian the most beautiful language, Italian food the most delicious, Italians the best singers, Italians the best, the only teachers of singing; that Italians were *simpatico*.

(Germans on the other hand were ugly, the German language hideous and no good for singing, German food ghastly. German opera—apart from Mozart and anyway he was Austrian and wrote Italian opera—ruined the voice, Wagner ruined the voice, German teachers ruined the voice. Germans were not *simpatico*.)

Ah, but the Italians . . . .

My mother was a great favourite with the Italians. They called her *Fioretta* because she was like a little flower. Who would want to be Clever if they could be *Fioretta*?

Our minds were full of wierd scraps of information and phrases out of her past.

"Who was it Blushed Up Crimson, Mum?"

"That was my friend Fanny Peden, when we were living in Newtown. She was a terrible giggler. She was always having adventures with young men. 'Florrie,' she would say. 'I was standing on the corner of Bond Street with You-know-who, and *he squeezed my hand*! Ooh! I *Blushed Up Crimson*!' Amy said she had no brains. They were very poor in those days. Now Fanny's brother's a *great* swell. Sir John Peden. But I always liked Fanny . . . ."

Though many of my parents' youthful friends had become distinguished—writers, artists, poets, lawyers, surgeons—they were known to us children privately and disrespectfully by their christian names and often by long-discarded idiosyncracies. My mother was mainly responsible for this, with her eye for absurdities and her habit of seeing people forever at the age when she first knew them.

"Tell about *Awfly Pretty Mounted on Red Plu-hush*, Mum," we would cry, imitating her throaty impersonation of a bashful suitor. "Tell about *Good Gawd, look at Claude!*"

She recited dramatically, getting much of her effects from long pauses and emphasis on odd words, in odd places.

"Well . . . HERbert Curlewis had a very shy brother called Claude. Wore boots. Never came to our parties. Too shy. Oh, those PARties! Lancers in the old kitchen! They said he was sweet on ME!"

At the dreamy look in her eye, fearful she might wander off the track we would bark, "Go on . . . go on!"

"We were so terribly POOR. Thirteen children! And our mother never seemed to worry about the house. Too busy. Immersed in BOOKS. And Louie and Amy always writing. No one noticed but me. I was always trying to imPROVE things. I would spend all my pocket-money. PATHETIC! I bought ferns. I cut up my dresses and petticoats to make lampshades. I mended the curtains and dyed them in coffee. I draped the mantelpiece with serge . . . ."

"*Serge?*"

"Very fashionable in those days. But it never did much good. A drop-in-the-bucket."

"The party, Mum, the party."

"Well . . . We were having a PARty. Herbert came and brought Claude. The FIRST time he'd come to the house. There we all were in the drawingroom . . . your FATHER was there too . . . talking and laughing. Then . . . ALL OF A SUDDEN . . ."

Pause.

"Suddenly CLAUDE, sitting there in a corner. He flung up his arms and toppled over on to the floor!"

"The chair!"

"Everyone turned round and STARED. *Poor Claude . . .*"

"The chair!" we urged, lest she choke with her giggles. "The chair!"

"And then, Herbert . . . HERbert drawled out at the TOP

39

of his voice: *Good Gawd, look at Claude*! And everyone STARED!"

Pause.

"Poor Claude was SCARLET. He must have wished the ground would open-and-swallow-him-up!"

"It was you!"

"Yes! It was ME! I did it! I put a log of wood under the chair. The leg was broken. I was always trying to fix things in the house . . . ." She leaned about, weeping with laughter. "He tried to move the chair forward . . . the log ROLLED OUT BEFORE EVERYONE. THUMP . . . THUMP . . . THUMP. Right into the MIDDLE OF THE FLOOR!

"Lou was *furious*. She said, 'I bet that's Florrie!' and of course it was. And Louie put that chair into her FIRST book, *The World is Round*."

"What happened to Claude?"

"Never came again! Never! That was the end of him. Oh, but the parties. We used to dance in the old kitchen. The Lancers . . . ."

She would push back her chair, fling out her arms and swoop diagonally across our kitchen, humming and singing and calling directions: "Ladies on the right. Gentlemen on the left. Join your partners. Ladies' chain. Ah! When I THINK! I had a dress of GREY NUNSVEILING. Never had more than one dress. NOT like YOU girls . . . ."

"How did you manage to have parties if your father was so strict?"

"TERribly strict. Dancing was forBIDDEN. We had them when he was away. And once he went to Europe. Louie and Amy and their friends. Sid and his university friends . . . Herbert Curlewis and Jim Pickburn and Arthur Kelynack and John Meillion — and YOUR FATHER . . .

"Billy Creagh! Sid brought him home. Oh, your father was handsome! Such beautiful hair . . . thick, glossy, wavy black hair. And beautifully-made small hands and feet. And the most BEAUTIFUL DANCER! Of course he didn't notice *me*!

He was very taken with Aunty Alice. She was SO pretty. Big dark eyes and lovely complexion. We were ALL pretty little things. With beautiful hair and complexions. WE didn't burn ourselves up on the beach the way YOU GIRLS do. Only Ame. She was sallow, always sallow. But ALL the boys liked her. Oh, she was popular. She was so merry and mischievous. You remember Brenda, in *Teens*? That was Ame."

"What about Dad and Aunty Alice?"

"He took her to a BALL at the Yacht Club. White gloves. He had a cold. Alice said he SNIFFED all the time. A most BEAUTIFUL dancer, your father . . . ."

Now she was gliding round the room singing a Viennese waltz.

"Then why did he marry you if he liked Aunty Alice?"

"It was the music . . . the MUSIC. He loved music . . ."

This sudden taking-off was quite usual. She would put down the cup or dish she held and, arms outstretched, go waltzing round the kitchen, sometimes when stirred by a record but often just for the mood. Crying, "Oh Music! Music!" away she would go. We did not think it strange. We frequently did it ourselves.

Our aunt Louise was the chief heroine of my mother's inaccurate, prejudiced, absorbing stories. As a result of her biased pride in this sister we regarded her as a genius.

"Tell about Aunty Louie writing *Teens*."

"Well . . . THERE she was, a little schoolgirl. Upstairs, writing her book on the corner of the washstand."

"Why was she writing it on the washstand?"

"BeCAUSE there were THIRteen boys and girls and no ROOM TO SPARE. When I think of our diningroom table, with thirteen little heads round it . . . and our Mother and Father . . . .

"*Teens*. She put us all in. And she dedicated it to us. *From the Sister who led you into so many scrapes.* Blue Eyes, Grey Eyes—that's me; Brown Eyes—Aunty Alice. Black Eyes. Amy was Black Eyes."

"Who's Blue Eyes? There's no Blue Eyes."

"Gert. Dimsie."

"But Dimsie's got *green eyes!*"

"Oh be quiet, you little pest. Don't be so sharp."

But she could never resist going on.

"Lou was writing upstairs in her bedroom on the corner of the washstand and Ethel was writing too. Eth-el TUR-ner! A little FAIR English girl. Ah! Those days, at the Sydney Girls' High School! You remember in *Teens* how Lennie Leighton—that was Lou—was running a school magazine and another girl started a rival paper called *The Bluebell*? That was Ethel. But it was really called *The Iris*. Ethel was *so* pretty. Such a pretty little thing, fair hair and blue eyes. *Flowwie*, she always called me; couldn't pronounce her Rs. Flowwie. I was always fond of Ethel."

We saw Ethel Turner forever sixteen, blue-eyed and fair-haired. She had no more connection with the lady we knew as Mrs Curlewis, though she still said *Flowwie*, who was written about in the papers as an Authoress than poor Claude's brother Herbert had with the stern and dignified Judge Curlewis.

"Was Ethel the one who said, 'Flowwie, tell me how to make sthphonge-cake'?"

"No, that was Mrs Curlewis, Herbert's *Mother*. They were so poor. I liked Mrs Curlewis. Always in a muddle. *Run out and get a cake of soap, Gertie wants to wash her hands.*"

"Go on about Ethel."

"ETH-el MARRied HERbert CurLEWis."

"No no, about the books."

"Oh, YOU know what happened," she would say, cross at our needling, and make moves to get up. "Little pests! Louie wrote *Teens*, Ethel wrote *Seven Little Australians* . . . . Louie was NO GOOD AT BUSINESS. She took her book to George Robertson and sold it for TEN POUNDS!"

"What did Ethel do?"

"She sent hers to London, to Ward Lock. Poor Lou!"

"Why did she only get ten pounds?"

"Because she wanted to go to ENGland. You could go steerage for ten pounds in those days. Angus & Robertson made hundreds out of *Teens*. But she didn't get a PENNY. She SOLD THE COPYRIGHT! They told her the book wouldn't sell. It sold for YEARS!"

We saw it all . . . the schoolgirl writing late at night on the washstand, selling her book for a pittance and going steerage to London without a penny while the villainous publisher lived it up on the fortune made from her royalties. It was with disappointment that we heard the true story from our Aunt Amy, who not only liked Mr Robertson but disapproved of her sister Louise.

"So Lou went to LONdon!" Pause. Pique forgotten, my mother stood entranced at the memory. "And she STARVED in a GARRET in BLOOMSBURY. And wrote fifteen novels. And became the FIRST WOMAN WAR CORRESPON-DENT FOR Lord NORTHcliffe. And W. T. Stead, Editor of the *Review of Reviews*, took a GREAT fancy to her. He was a spiritualist, you know, he used to have seances. He gave your Aunt Alice a photograph of himself sitting beside THE GHOST OF CECIL RHODES! Of course they said it was faked. He went down in the *Titanic*. He was SO good to Louie. He used to have her down there at his house to dinner. All the Intellectuals of London and these TWO little girls in their simple white DRESSES . . . Louie and Alice. Alice went over to stay with Louie in London. She wrote stories but she gave it up when she got married. All sorts of people! What a wonderful time! Went everywhere . . . knew everyone . . . ."

Louie in London, Louie in Belgium, in disguise, hiding from the Germans, Louie in Italy, editing a paper in Florence . . . but always the stories came back to Louie the ringleader, the marvellous elder sister.

"Lou used to bring girls home in the middle of the NIGHT after BALLS and make us give up our beds. I often had to sleep on the FLOOR or get in with Amy. I used to BLUSH because I KNEW there were never enough clean towels or pillowcases. Lou didn't care. Once I heard a girl saying piteously, 'Louie, can I have a pillowcase?' *I* knew there weren't any; but Lou wasn't embarrassed. She said witheringly, *'What do you want a pillowcase for? Don't be such an old maid!'*"

And my mother would giggle and wipe her eyes and sigh for that wonderful time of lilacs.

6

Killarney

UNTIL the year of our Aunt Amy's return, life was centred in our garden with my brother John, a soft Nordic Buddha, the sort of infant people stop in the street to admire. Regularly, at my mother's proud behest, from table tops, from white bear-skins, in knitted coats, holding rabbits or wooden engines, he gazed into photographers' lenses with the clear candid blue regard that never changed all through his short life.

We were inseparable. As soon as he was mobile I manoeuvred him into mischief, hauling him up into trees, sliding him down over cliffs, dragging him through bushes. He followed without question, trustfully doing my bidding. Perhaps he sensed he would not be blamed, that that was my prerogative. As we grew older it was he who defended me from the punishments I had earned for us both.

Now, we were to be parted. He must remain in the garden, eating clay, a taste he had learnt from me, while I went with Sheila to school.

For my mother, the preliminary interview some weeks before with Miss Grant, the school's owner and principal, had been a formality. Not only was Sheila an established pupil; everyone knew everyone else. Miss Grant's sister lived at the foot of our hill, married to a solicitor known to my father. For me it was less formality than ordeal. Chronically guilty, I felt Miss Grant

45

disapproved of me. Pale, dark-eyed, handsome, strict, just, a gentlewoman, from the very beginning she had the power to make me feel my underwear was not quite up to scratch, my nails not quite clean.

The school was conducted downstairs in the old Grant house. In a corner of the lawn tennis-court facing the quiet street a notice said:

KILLARNEY
SCHOOL FOR GIRLS AND
KINDERGARTEN

At that time, Mosman had only Killarney and The Infants at the Public School. The Public School kids, we were told, were cheeky, common and verminous. We, they rightly claimed, were stuck-up.

Now that hard beginnings, rough schooling are so esteemed, my childhood appears pampered and effete. So much beauty surrounded me, so much sun and freedom, and I enjoyed it all so completely. I did not suffer at school; from the moment I entered Killarney gates at the age of five I was enslaved by the old house, its gardens and high-ceilinged rooms, its haunting atmosphere of grace and elegance.

Built perhaps in the 1880s, it stood in large grounds among fine trees. It was not beautiful, in the classic Georgian sense, but there was grandeur and dignity in its red-gravelled drive, square Italianate tower, iron lace on the upstairs balconies, tiled verandas and French windows. Behind was a stable-yard with old redbrick stables and carriage-house. The two school-rooms were large, lofty, with white marble mantelpieces. One room was papered tobacco-brown, the other bottle-green.

Whatever schooling I had at Killarney was subsidiary to the setting, the green lawns and tennis court, roses and jasmin-hung summer-house. As with the bay, it now seems to have always been summer, a world scented with pittosporum and garden flowers, of fine parched grass, plumbago hedges powdered with pale dust, of drowsiness and delicious struggle to keep awake in the dim shaded room while the heat pulsated outside and cicadas drummed in the camphor laurels.

Education, in any case, was not very complex. The Juniors, in the green room, had plasticine, raffia, cutting-out and pasting-in; the Big Girls, in the brown room, had sums and High Roads of History. You stayed at Killarney till you were ten, then went to Redlands or one of the Church of England Girls Grammar Schools. The little boys moved on rather earlier to Mosman Prep.

At one side of the house, part of the veranda had been enclosed for a cloak-room. Here we left hats and coats, entering the class-rooms through the French windows. The front door and hall, Miss Grant's private section, were out of bounds.

I longed to explore this hall, large, dark and shiny, to sit there alone feeling the silence, smelling the scent of old polished furniture, strangely moved and disturbed in a way I could not understand by the vast staircase with carved posts and the stained-glass landing window filtering muted light. On the right was the heavy door of the drawingroom and a passage led off through a green baize door to stone-flagged kitchen quarters.

For the pupils, the hall, the drawingroom, the forbidden parts of the house were associated with illness, emergency, bad news, disaster. Only these qualified us for admittance; yet when, found to have chickenpox, I was isolated in the drawing-room until called for, my pleasure was overshadowed by shame and guilt.

"How *could* your mother have LET you come to school!" Miss Grant had said, shocked, so I felt it was all my fault; and when my mother arrived she too seemed to blame me because the spots had come out after I left home.

The only way to really enjoy the hall and drawingroom was to be an object of sympathy, the innocent victim of a fall or a bad cut with blood. At such times Miss Grant's mother came with basins of water and boracic acid and one was enclosed in soft compassionate murmurs. Once, being hit on the head by a swing, I was even taken upstairs to a gigantic bathroom with olive-green and white flowering tiles and enormous mahogany W.C.

Those who were old enough to stay at school all day ate their sandwiches in the garden, on benches by the plumbago hedge, beneath the camphor laurels or by the swings and bars, where after lunch one hung by the legs, full of jam sandwiches and water from the bubbler. The privileged Big Girls ate in the summer-house with latticed walls threaded with jasmine. This building became the setting for every garden proposal scene in every historical romance I read in my teens.

As the school prospered and grew, extra classrooms were made in the stables and coach-house. I longed to be old enough for this romantic world of white-washed arches, hand-made brick and courtyard pump where old Mrs Grant washed out with soap and water the mouths of pupils caught telling lies. I was incredulous when girls said their parents objected to their being taught in A Stable.

Every year we had sports on the tennis court with egg-and-spoon race and sack-race and relay races and afternoon tea, brought by the pupils. Parents walked about on the lawns and the air smelt of fresh-cut grass and egg sandwiches.

End-of-year Breaking-up was in Mosman Town Hall—singing, elocuting, artistic dancing in butter-muslin, tableaux in crinkle-paper, even plays in cotton-wool wigs and sateen crinolines. The stage was decorated with white shasta daisies and blue hydrangeas whose very smell was exciting, so closely connected with summer. Generals, Mayors or Bishops made speeches telling us we couldn't all win prizes; but we did. It was the policy of the school. They were given for Improvement, Good Conduct, Attendance and similar merits.

At John's first Breaking-up concert he and I sang a duet taught us at home by my mother, a bowdlerized version of Shakespeare's Spring Song:

When dai-hai-sies pied, and vi-o-lets blue
And lai-hai-hai-dy-smocks all si-hi-hil-ver white,
And cuck-oo buds of ye-hell-low hue,
Do paint the me-hea-dows wi-hith de-light,
The cuckoo, then *on* ev-er-*y* tree,
Hails *the sweet spring,* hails *the sweet spring,*
HAILS the sweet SPRING
   And —— thus —— sings —— HEEEEEEEE . . .
Cuckoo! Cuckooooo! Coooookoooooo. . . .

"How sweet," the audience murmured, smiling sentimentally at our fair hair, our pink and white faces.

When she-he-perds pipe on o-ho-ten straws,
And me-he-he-ry larks are plow-how-how-men's clocks,
When tur-tles pair and roo-hooks and daws
And fields are sca-ha-tered aw-hawl with flocks,
The cuckoo. . . .

Following our mother's instructions we dwelt on the cuckoo, at first happily, then with a slight unease as the audience began to show amusement. We had come to the end of the last prolonged *Cuckoo* but as I opened my mouth for the next line, John uttered, high and clear, another bird call.

"*Cuckoo!*"

The audience started to laugh. I glared at them, angry and harrassed, for John, I could see, was panicking. He was glancing round nervously with the expression of one about to forget his words.

"*Cuckoo! Cuckoo! Cooo-koooo!*" he sang, appealing for help.

The accompanist had gone on. I raced to catch up:

"*Oh, pleasing sound! Oh, PLEASING sound. . . .*" but I could not drown out my brother. Growing redder, his eyes filled with frightened tears he sang on desperately:

"*Cuckooo! Cuckoooo! Cooooo. . . .*"

The audience roared. I raised my voice, almost shouting:

49

While E-he-he-co answers fro-ho-hom the hill,
While E-he-co ah-hahn-swers fro-hom the hill. . . .

"Cuckoo! Oh *Damn and Blast!*" cried John with a burst of angry tears and ran from the stage.

Our Junior mistress encouraged the telling of tales, rewarding with favour the most gifted spies. When I moved into Miss Grant's class I was quickly disillusioned.

"Miss Grant," I said virtuously, raising my hand. "Maisie's eating."

Instead of saying, "Thank you, dear," as Miss C. would have done, Miss Grant said very coldly, "I always think the tale-bearer worse than the one who is told upon."

I sat down, scarlet, baffled at such inconsistency.

I was learning fast that adults were not to be trusted. Only recently, on Miss Grant's instruction, I had asked my mother to buy me a new box of crayons. Each day she promised, each day forgot. Each day Miss Grant grew more cool and severe. When I once more besought my mother she said impatiently, "Well, I can't get them today. I haven't got any money."

Glad at last to be able to give a reason, I confided this fact to Miss Grant. She looked odd and said in a tight voice, "I see!" Instead of approval, my mother showed outrage.

They were all incomprehensible. You could never do the right thing with them, even my adored Junior mistress, a beautiful ravishing creature in transparent muslin blouses through which you saw camisoles with lace insertions and pink or blue ribbons. She was really a pallid blonde with faded hair in a bun, light blueish eyes and not very good teeth with gold fillings. She had a pale oily skin and a large reddish nose with rather big pores, but to me she was a goddess. Told one day we might draw what we liked, I chose my idol.

"What are you drawing, dear?" asked Miss M., leaning over my shoulder.

I said, "I'm drawing Miss C."

I wasn't much of an artist but I had laboured to faithfully reproduce every detail. I was hurt and bewildered when Miss M. angrily snatched up my picture.

"You're a horrible, rude little girl!" she said. "I'll tell Miss C."

I sat stunned while she tore up the profile I had so carefully drawn, with prominent rose-crayoned nose on which every enlarged pore was lovingly marked like a strawberry.

7

Salt Horse and Sea Biscuits

ON the walls of my father's study were photographs of Sayonara Cup crews, in which he sailed five times, dashing in white polo-necked sweaters and yachting caps, arms folded, on the steps of the Yacht Club at Kirribilli; or in brass buttons with Jellicoe caps pushed back, knees crossed, knuckles resting negligently upon hips. In these pictures he looked young, handsome, debonair; but when he took us sailing he dressed rather differently.

"Like a Portuguese fisherman!" my mother would say despairingly.

He would reply caustically, "Do you expect me to dress myself up like a Veranda Admiral just to go for a sail?"

My mother had not been in Portugal, where fishermen dress rather gaily; her ideas came from Portuguese families down at The Spit, in ramshackle houseboats or brine-smelling hovels among the lantana and rocks of Pearl Bay. Their dressing was casual indeed but nothing to touch my father's boating outfits.

The smartest comprised grey flannels hacked off half-way up the calves with a pen-knife, an old waistcoat laced on with cord, a mouldy panama hat with a line run under the chin for stiff breezes. Even more striking was the two-piece swimming-gear, with drawers that drooped down the calves and a sleeveless overblouse, like a shift, that hung to the knees. It was stiffened and almost white with dried salt and went with a felt hat and sunglasses mended with bent pins and wire.

Devoid of self-consciousness, my father would appear so attired in full daylight on fashionable beaches. Though an arrant beach-snob in my teens I could never resist the joy of these manifestations, the Churchillian disregard for public opinion. As Edith Sitwell wrote of Squire Waterton: "He was an eccentric only as all great gentlemen are eccentric, by which I mean that their gestures are not born to fit the conventions or the cowardice of the crowd."

Once we were able to swim we could be taken out in the boat, at first mainly for picnics. We would sail to Quarantine Beach or Castle Rock across the bay, drop anchor and rig up an awning over the cockpit. Sometimes we stayed on board for lunch, sometimes picnicked ashore.

While my mother was rowed in with the food baskets we would struggle into our swimming costumes, to lose not a moment, impatient for the dinghy to come back. This coffin-shaped craft had been christened *Mrs P. Kirby*, by my father, after a Sydney undertaker.

I loved the moment of going ashore, when all the concentrated heat came out from the land to meet you, when you climbed into the shallows to drag the boat up and sniffed the smell of hot sand and sour seaweed and rotting unmentionables behind the rocks, of lantana and woodsmoke. Then came the rush to the water, the rush to the food, the light from the sand glaring up, the reflected heat burning the face.

Better still was to stay aboard when the awning was up; or row back alone in *Mrs P. Kirby* and stretch on the deck in the shade, cooled by a gentle breeze, trailing a hand in the water, gazing into the depths, longing to let oneself over the side and sink down into them, while beyond, the dazzling glare on the sea, the shimmering heat intensified present comfort and ease.

Such activities gained attraction because they were not approved. Children did not lie about in the shade, they ran and swam; it was frightfully bad form to trail your hand in the

53

water, as bad as wearing shoes in a boat; and you were not allowed to let yourself over the side because of sharks.

Lunch at these picnics was not sophisticated. My father would have fed us the food of windjammers, salt-horse and sea-biscuits, but though my mother obediently provided the corned beef she also brought salad and sausage pie, soda loaf, cakes, scones, fruit and billy tea.

After lunch, swimming was forbidden for an hour. While my mother dozed in the shade my father, with trousers rolled up, would stand ankle-deep in the water and gaze out to sea, partly meditating, partly watching the sailing of other boats with a critical eye. Bloated with food, we children sunbaked, climbed the rocks, paddled about in the dinghy or went for a sail with my father, returning for four o'clock tea.

Though Castle Rock was not far—we could see our own beach, our house across the water—it was enchanted country, untouched, inaccessible by land. Round the next green headland was Clontarf, where atoll-white sand gently merged into smooth clear shallows, and gnarled bottle-brush trees, like ancient olives, basked in the enduring light of mellow rich afternoons.

These Treasure Island beaches were the white crescents we could see from our house; the flat rough grass beyond Clontarf was the home of gypsyish campers whose cries and bugles I heard in the night. It was here that Queen Victoria's son, the Duke of Edinburgh, was shot at. In later days two Egyptian temples were built on opposite sides of the narrow strait, one at Clontarf, one at The Spit. My father led us, gasping with fear, through the vast submarine pipe where the sewerage water would flow, to the opening in the Clontarf hillside, where as in a coal mine, little trucks on railway lines came out full of earth, and slow oozings trickled down damp clay walls, filling the air with cold, claustrophobic smells.

Sometimes we went further afield, to the little beach below the Quarantine Station on North Head, halfway to Manly. It was my father's favourite and to us always tinged with adventure. From here, our after-lunch promenades were taken Outside the Heads. These sorties into the open Pacific brought the wildest excitement, the sense of Polynesian voyagers setting forth.

Almost invariably we had Castle Rock and Clontarf to ourselves; Quarantine was loved and frequented by yachtsmen. Its quiet air echoed the small rattle of anchor chains, its sheltered bay reflected white moving hulls. Dinghies splashed ashore, voices called from boat to boat. It was rather a family affair since most of the yachtsmen knew each other; yet the little beach retained a curious secrecy. It may have been the close embrace of its protecting hills, its loop-shaped bay, or perhaps because it faced west.

Beaches that watch the sun set have an essence rarely found in those looking east. They are lagoon beaches, warm, drowsy, full of stored richness. No winds blow from the sea to disperse their magic, no waves break on their sands to disturb their dreams.

Quarantine-Castle-Rock picnics were kindergarten, soft stuff with women and children, a preliminary conditioning for serious sailing. Soon we moved on to going out with our Uncle Albert, in *Ianthe*. He never took women or baskets of food. There were rather dull sandwiches and a silent man who coiled ropes. He was called Mr Idriess. Withdrawn, even gloomy, he never talked. We were astounded when he turned out to be a writer. The authors we knew were not silent at all.

Uncle Albert and Mr Idriess were two of a kind where the boat was concerned, disapproving of idle chatter, dropped crumbs, messing about. On relaxed days we sailed mutely to a given point, ate our sandwiches, had a brief swim, then sailed again. On proper sailing days, when the boats were racing, children did not come.

Though our own first boat, a cadet dinghy 12ft long and rather broad in the beam, came when I was about twelve, we were not allowed to actually sail her till we had mastered all the more menial chores . . . knowing the names of each part of the boat, putting the sails on the spars, taking them off, lashing and lacing, reefing, hosing out, drying and stowing away. We had to learn how to bale, how to come alongside, raise and lower the centre-board for going ashore, lean outboard and inboard and look sharp nipping under the boom when the boat went about. Even after we graduated in these arts we rarely touched the tiller. We must first work as for'ard hand, which also meant lowering the jib without letting it droop in the water, handling the spinnaker, casting off from and picking up the moorings without falling overboard. We took turns as for'ard hand or in sitting in the bottom of the boat holding the main sheet, a dull job with no scope for action because my father, at the tiller, when not giving precise commands and instructions, leaned over and took the sheet himself, leaving you nothing to do.

For'ard hand was different; it meant leaning outboard with legs locked round the thwart, dodging and crouching, waiting while we went about, feeling the boat's movement in one's own body, trying to predict what she would do next, snatching at wet sheets while my father bawled, "Get that jib in! Do you want everyone to think I'm out with a boat full of mugs?"

When we passed his sailing friends in their big boats they would laugh and call, "Take that boat home, Billy. Do you want to be drowned?"

We soon knew every boat by name and sight, every part of the harbour, each beach and headland, navigation light and channel. We were experts on Sydney yachting history and the rules of sailing. When we were old enough to go out without my father we would dare bigger boats to run us down, frisking round racing yachts, even Manly ferries, shouting, "Give way! Rule of the road!"

This was forbidden; so was sailing alongside the handsome *Boomerang* playing imaginary mouth-organs. *Boomerang's* owner, whose money came from a music shop and Boomerang mouth-organs, was a foreigner who had Anglicized his name. In conservative circles he was viewed with reserve, less for being foreign and in trade than because he paid someone to sail his boat.

As well as our thorough grounding in sailing—theoretical, practical, historical—we had to prove ourselves good sailors. My father would take us out to the entrance between the Heads where, in sweltering heat and a sickening swell, the sails were dropped and we were fed condensed milk, sardines, bananas and cold Christmas pudding. If we survived, we passed the test.

As we rolled and lurched and chewed my father would entertain us.

"That's where the *Dunbar* went down," he would say, waving at South Head and the Gap. "No, *that's* where the *Dunbar* went down!"

This never failed to cheer us, no matter how wan our smiles. Waving wildly at the rocky cliffs we would respond, "No, *that's* where the *Dunbar* went down!"

I am not quite sure why this was funny, since the *Dunbar* sank with terrible loss of life; it was vaguely connected with Henry Lawson . . . a story of himself or a New Zealander being shown the spot by eager fellow-passengers; but it was one of our family jokes. We were also beguiled with tales of the sea, excerpts from Dickens, Thackeray, Mark Twain, Josh Billings, Barry Pain, and lines from Norman Lindsay's *Magic Pudding*, Gilbert's *Bab Ballads* and the Latin poets. You never knew whether you were going to be treated to:

> *Chopped shallot, which he never forgot,*
> *And sage and parsley too . . .*

or

> *Eheu fugaces, Postume, Postume,*
> *labuntur anni nec pietas moram . . .*

or

> *Whiskers alone are bad enough*
> *Attached to faces coarse and rough.*
> *But how much greater their offence is*
> *When stuck on Uncles' countenances.*

It was a matter of honour with some of my family to get back to the moorings under sail, even without wind. Lacking this kind of pride I would shiver, with chattering teeth and rats-tail hair, while the less proud, more fortunate swept past on the end of tow-ropes. Friendly offers of assistance were always refused with an airy wave. There would be a puff in a minute that would take us right in.

On hot evenings it was no hardship to sit, licking salt from the lips, the whole skin stiff and powdered with dried spray, in a sea like glass with an orange sun going down behind purple clouds and voices echoing across the water. Sometimes night fell before the moorings were reached, the moon rose and we floated beside our own silver ghosts. People sang softly and sadly and lights shone out from the hills; then the sea mist would rise and cut us off from the earth and one felt on the threshhold of a stupendous mystery.

At these times the final manoeuvres, the stowing away, the hosing and spreading of sails to dry would be carried out silently. In silence you moved from the tar-and-latrine-smelling boatshed into the hot still night with its scent of pleasant dust and dark shapes of Moreton Bays against stars.

At other times, becalmed beneath an overcast sky, goose-fleshed and chafed in wet clothes, you wondered why you continued to suffer this misery. Pitting your strength against the wind, with back arched out over flying-past water and waves crashing into your face was supreme happiness; this wet ignominious straggling back was anti-climax.

Yet the worse the discomfort the more one enjoyed the contrast of home: the feeling of weariness washing away, of aching muscles and petrified limbs relaxing in the hot shower; the soft mattress, the tray brought upstairs—"*You'll all have pneumonia! Can't THINK what Dad's doing, taking you out in such weather!*" Then, from the warm secure bed, looking down on the bay, now deserted, grown dark and forbidding, and drifting to sleep with a faint cradle-rocking sensation.

The joys of white hulls against blue seas, white sails against blue skies, of techniques and jargon and boat talk were balanced by more subtle pleasures: awareness of danger and complete security because my father was at the tiller; looking up in the teeth of a gale at our house on the hill where my mother was making rock-cakes in a warm dry kitchen; the comfort of home after turbulent seas, of stillness after storm.

8

A Little Bit of Sauce-a

THOUGH sailing was confined to summer, the boat was always present, in conversation, in maintenance chores, in certain domestic observances. In our family, pulleys and ropes were called blocks and tackle; vehicles, even people, were said to get under way or go astern. Sea shanties were sung as hymns might be in a more devout household. A frustrated Crusoe, my father was always prepared for the emergency, the desert island, the big blow. Whenever possible he wore sandshoes. Unlike other fathers, when it rained he went into oilskins and sou-wester; and though the boat was up on the slips for the winter he still liked to use the special tea-kit he had assembled for sailing. This consisted of old rusty biscuit tins, lined with floor-felt and fitted with marmite and Fruit Salts jars, bottles and a thermos, all in their own felt jackets, sewn in waxed thread by himself with a sailor's needle and palm. In the off-season this became equipment for nocturnal snacks.

Tea-making was always a source of dissension between my parents. My mother believed it should be brewed in a tea-pot, silver for preference, but my father felt it was only drinkable made as billy tea. His method was to boil the water in a sauce-pan, cast in a generous handful of tea leaves and bubble them fast until he got a mixture black as tar. Milk was thrown in, the potion boiled up again, then left to mature till needed, when it would be reheated at a great rate for immediate use or for storing in the thermos.

My mother never knew which saucepan would be used, for the billy was usually boiled late at night while she slept. Eventually all were irrevocably stained black, inside and out.

If my father became absorbed elsewhere the tea would boil away, the saucepan turn red, the house smell of molten metal and silver aluminium tears splash out all over the stove. My mother would say, "Really, dear!" We thought it deliciously funny.

Normally my father never went into the kitchen, except to thrust saucepans aside and put soldering-irons into the flames, but occasionally if my mother were sick and there was no domestic to keep him at bay he would invade, quivering with eagerness for experiment. In the cause of science he would throw salt on gas jets so they burned green, demonstrate new time-and-motion economies in washing up, making us count our steps between sink and dresser; sometimes even create new gourmet treats. Most of these, such as *Pa's Patent Porridge*, made a great mess, caused shrieks of laughter and several burnt saucepans.

This sort of thing did not make it easy to keep servants. Not till his old age did my father encounter someone who could accept his ways. It took the long Russian view of mortality, the warm Slav heart and instinct for first things first to give perspective to his eccentricities.

"Ah!" Valya would say compassionately. "Your *dedushka* is such a wonderful old man. *So clean!*"

But in the Slavless days of my childhood his peculiarities were a serious obstacle to my mother's half-ashamed longings for order and outward appearances. Though she had been among erratics and nonconformists from birth and glibly spoke their tongue, she was not wholeheartedly one of them. Secretly she pined for meals on time, maids in frilled caps and aprons and a household where unexpected visitors did not involve the hasty slamming of doors.

Unfortified by her sisters' Bohemianism, her husband's lofty detachment, she expressed her frustrated despair in the cry that no decent servant would stay.

It was true. If one came by mistake she soon took herself off, to universal relief. We found it just too much effort to live up to these paragons of gentility, though I was always eager to hear their stories of former employers—millionaires to a man—and the high life. Even my mother's chagrin and disappointment would be lightened by reprieve from the fear of what we might do to displease or shock the Treasure. So, until hope sprang once more in her breast, we would return to the only sort of domestic that would tolerate us . . . girls with mysterious pasts, deserted wives, half-mad spinsters, agile pensioners.

The more peculiar the past, the more eccentric the character, the better we children were pleased. There was a warm rapport between us and the bedroom next to the kitchen, where the window was always shut tight and the air smelt of cheap stale powder, corsets and unwashed stockings kept under the eiderdown, hair-combings, dandruff, feet, and jerries maturing in bedside cupboards. I would spend hours crouched on the bed watching the current occupant squeezing into her stays or powdering her face. It charmed because forbidden, because it was alien to our world of cold showers and well-ventilated security; because I sensed Events beyond my experience, a grown-up side of life from which we were shielded.

I also spent a good deal of time in the kitchen, when my mother was out, listening. The kitchen was large and high-ceilinged and from the back door you could see the blue bay. In one wall was a discarded fuel stove and over the pantry door—large as a modern bedroom—an oblong box faced with black and gilt glass. Six little circular windows revealed beautiful lettering. *Front door. Drawingroom. Diningroom. First Bedroom. Second Bedroom. Third Bedroom.* If you pressed the bell in the drawingroom and then ran fast enough you could catch the *Drawingroom* lettering flipping eagerly back and forth. Such attractions were beguiling but it was for conversation that I haunted the kitchen. I was the main student of sleaziness. John lacked interest, Sheila was less gullible. I understood little but feared to say so. Trying to look comprehending, I restrained any instinct to question lest I be dismissed as too young.

"And *mind!*" the story would always conclude. "Don't you tell your mother I told you this! She said I wasn't to talk to you about such things."

Such things were sex and violence, hatred and drunkenness, petty crime and betrayal, squalor, fear, misery and despair, as strange, frightening and irresistible as scraps of sensational newspapers accidently encountered, or sinister posters warning against some incomprehensible evil in noisome railway lavatories.

My pretence of intelligent understanding deprived me of explanations, and impressions were mainly confused; but lack of technical knowledge did not stop me receiving the essence. Frightened, I came back for more, inexplicably aware that this was just as important, as much part of life as the beauties and pleasures that occupied most of our lawful existence.

It was real yet not real. Though it happened to others it could not happen to Us. In our world little brothers did not choke slowly to death before your eyes, fathers did not hit mothers with broken bottles, husbands did not come home drunk and beat up their families, mothers did not run away with other men and leave their children to starve, people didn't have fits in the tram or go mad and pull off all their clothes in the street; death-rattles, layings-out, anguished screams, mourners throwing themselves into open graves did not occur. Callously, blandly secure I longed to be an observer of such fearful scenes.

Once or twice drama flickered wonderfully close . . . an unbalanced spinster's account of imaginary rape, a maid coming home at 4 a.m. with a cock-and-bull tale of a brother drowned at The Spit, a drunken girl having hysterics. I do not know how we learnt of these events, they certainly were not described to us. We heard sounds, words, scraps, we eavesdropped on our mother's telephone conversations, we guessed and were not put off by closed-up evasion or tales that the offender was sick. We knew what had happened when the maid's room became empty and my mother began advertising again.

The sinners were usually girls with thin hungry faces and disturbing eyes, who painted and powdered and tonged their hair on their day off and wore black lacy picture hats and spangles and transparent blouses. Their one interest was men, known as Boys. When not talking of their own, they questioned me about mine. In our household the term *Having a Boy* was considered vulgar and mothers who sentimentally paired-off young children were disapproved of. It was held that there was plenty of time for That. So the confidences always ended, "Don't you tell your mother . . . ."

But they weren't all sinners; there were also clowns. Mrs Faulkiner was a sad refined horse who put *A* on the end of most words. She plagued us so much with a previous employer's little daughter, Marjorie—straight from a Sunday school tract—that we took revenge in mimicking her curious speech behind her back. She also unwittingly drove my father to silent fury. No matter what he was eating she would appear at his side with a bottle of tomato sauce and say, "A little bit of sauce-A?"

At first he would refuse courteously, but soon was reduced to grinding his teeth and waving her away. She always came back.

"You are NOT to torment that poor creature!" my mother told us. "She is good and kind and unfortunate and a *gentlewoman*"; but she could not help laughing when Sheila offered a saucer, saying "A little bit of sauce-A?"

This cleverness was our downfall. Full of admiration for Sheila's wit, John took a saucer out to the kitchen next morning and said baldly, "Mrs Faulkiner, have a bit of saucer."

I had followed, giggling, to see the fun; but oh horror! There was no laughter, even rage. Mrs Faulkiner's mild sad eyes filled with tears, her equine face turned red. Stricken, we heard her say tremblingly, "You're very rude and cruel little children!" Even to hear, "*Marjorie* would never have done such a thing," did not help. In anguished embarrassment we fled; and such was our guilt hoped she would tell our mother so we could expiate in punishment.

Kind, injured, she kept silent; but as she continued to provoke my father with her now accursed question, it stabbed us, and probably her, each time she uttered it.

She went at last, back to Marjorie, I believe, leaving us with the new disturbing knowledge that grown-ups could be made to cry.

Edith Pearl Burrows was also destined to drive my father mad. Her form of persecution was to stand at the kitchen door on Sundays when he was hammering on the back veranda and scream, "Mr Creagh. What do you think I had better do about my divorce?"

"Can't you keep that wretched woman quiet?" he would fume at my mother; but nothing could quieten Edith Pearl. Her husband, Mr Austin, had deserted her, she confided to me over the ironing; never paid a penny maintenance, she hadn't seen him for years and even when she lived with him never supported her.

"And *mind* you don't tell your mother I told you all this. She said I wasn't to discuss my divorce with you."

Edith was plump with frizzed hair, false teeth that clacked, glasses, a fat stupid parrot-face with a permanent "Isn't it awful!" expression; but I found her a spell-binder. I hung on every word, leaning on the backs of kitchen chairs, helping fold endless sheets in order to hear the wondrous tale of her life with the defaulting Mr Austin.

"Burrows is my maiden name. No Tin about me," she said. I was convulsed.

She also talked of the state of her health. Her heart was

weak, she was likely to collapse at any minute for all sorts of reasons—mice, telegrams, smell of burning, sudden noises, brown eyes looking in through the window and so on. She screamed easily. Her nerves and sensibilities were such that she always wept, she said, at *God Save the King*, even in the theatre, while *Home Sweet Home* sent her off in a dead faint.

Though both Sheila and John were callously sceptical, I was deeply impressed and made sure this dangerous tune should never be played in her hearing.

One night when our parents had gone out to dinner, John perversely began to sing *Home Sweet Home*. Spurred on by my warnings and pleas he howled at the top of his voice.

"Don't! Don't! She'll faint. She'll have a heart attack!" I screamed in panic.

He sang louder.

I tried to stop him by force, we struggled and fought on the diningroom sofa but still he sang on. I awaited the scream, the thud in the kitchen announcing Edith's collapse, but John had finished and started again and still nothing stirred.

"Edith!" he shouted. "I'm singing *Home Sweet Home*!"

There was no reply.

"She's dead already!" I thought. "We've killed her!" I pictured her sprawled across the kitchen table, face-down in apple-pie, or perhaps lying cold on her bed. I burst into frightened tears and screamed at John, "You've killed her! You've killed her! She's dead!"

He stopped, alarmed at last.

"You go and see!" I cried. "She's out there, dead. I told you what she said, I told you not to sing it! You've killed her!"

He turned rather pale but stood up defiantly.

"You're mad!" he said, and went bravely out to the kitchen.

Edith Pearl, with spectacles on the end of her nose, was reading the paper. In her blue dress and white cap and apron she looked the picture of portly health.

"I knew it wasn't true!" John said scornfully, while I stared, shattered and disillusioned. "I knew it was a lie! I thought you said you'd faint dead away and have a heart attack if you heard *Home Sweet Home*! Well, I sang it, *twice*, and you never fainted."

Edith looked at him over her glasses and calmly said, "When I hear it played by a brass band, that's what makes me faint, a brass band." And she went on reading, unaware that she had driven yet another nail into the heart of my perishing trust in grown-ups.

9

Dipping In and Dipping Out

THE Harrisons, our Aunt Amy and Uncle Launce, had bought a house at Gordon. At that time most of the North Shore Line was unspoilt and they were close to bush walks down the gullies for watching birds and animals.

Without children of their own, they made do with nephews and nieces. Both had extraordinary insight and understanding of young minds and could reach them without effort.

Uncle Launce was a zoologist, which John and I thought meant he worked at the Zoo; but it turned out to be the university where he had a Chair. We pictured him sitting all day on a great wooden throne and wondered what he had done before he got it, if the university had only one chair and professors took turns or pounced when the music stopped and had to stand up at work if they missed.

The conversation of our elders often caused such confusions . . . someone on a Sabbatical; someone at the Bar; someone on the Bench; someone taking Silk; someone in chambers—this last always good for sniggers.

With children, Amy was warm, understanding, full of wonderful stories. It was hard sometimes to distinguish between those she made up specially for us and those we had read in her books, for she was always ready to invent sequels and further adventures. I had the idea that all the creatures she wrote about were her intimate friends, kept hidden away in her house, to be encountered unexpectedly, delightfully at any minute. Birds seen in her garden were never quite ordinary; there was always the chance they were out of *Bushland Stories* or *Scribbling Sue*.

"Is that Blue-cap, Aunty Amy? Is he going to his birthday party? . . . "Is that the Kookaburra who was so rude at the Birds' Concert?"

Amy always said "Yes". She made us laugh about the little fishes that defied big ones and Little Tits who were impudent to the big birds and we cried at the sad stories of the Little Wave and the White Herons.

Uncle Launce called her Ame; my mother called her Little Ame and we thought of her in some ways as being our own age. One night, listening to Caruso, she went into uncontrollable giggles.

"I caught a prawn!" she cried to my nonplussed parents. "He's saying *'I caught a prawn! I caught a prawn! Oh, one for the mother, one for the father, Oh, I caught a prawn!'"*

There was a quite different Amy for grown-ups, particularly for her sisters, an indignant, snorting, rather bossy little creature who made sweeping comments on people and literature and could with a word or glance demolish those she judged unworthy. "Your friends were always such *bores*, Flo!" she would say to my mother. "That Fanny Peden!" This Amy chain-smoked and drank black coffee and stayed up late reading and couldn't wake in the morning, unlike our fresh wholesome mother who went to bed at eight and rose at dawn. When you stayed at Gordon you had *hot baths* instead of the bracing showers our parents enforced all the year round. My mother was strongly critical of these effete habits which she put down to living in England where it was cold.

There were also two different Uncle Launces—The Perfesser and Alter Ego. Alter Ego wrote children's verses about birds and beasts, the Perfesser produced learned works on scientific subjects, but they were joint authors of a book for children called *Tails and Tarradiddles*. Many of its verses were written for our amusement and from them, as from Amy's stories, we painlessly learnt a good deal about Australian native creatures. We found it paralysingly funny that the Silvereye's real name is *Zosterops* and the Platypus is really *Ornithorhynchus*.

One of the attractions of going to stay at Gordon was that you went by train and on the way you could see Albert. Albert was a small privet-tree in a Chatswood backyard, visible from the train. It was trimmed to a perfect sphere and Uncle Launce had christened it after our dear *Magic Pudding*. So much did Albert mean to us that I still look for him instinctively as I pass. The Harrisons were marvellous at reading aloud *The Magic Pudding* and Lewis Carroll's *Alice* books. We doted upon them, mainly because the creatures were so often rude to each other.

Amy's house was full of books and old shiny furniture. The floors shone and there were the rugs we had seen that first morning, rolled up with the luggage. You could run and land on a rug and skate. There was also a grand piano and a four-poster bed which you walked up steps to get into. It had curtains with tiny birds and berries which Amy said were Liberty. The house smelt of books and flowers and log fires and claret and coffee. There was a garden full of flowers we didn't have at home, being too near the sea, and adjoining, a block of vacant land which Amy called The Wilderness and about which she wrote. It was never Improved. The wild birds and trees remained untouched.

There was also a cook called Sue, fat, red-faced and jovial. She wore a blue cotton dress and large white starched apron and made delicious gem scones, eaten hot, running with butter. She must have come from the country or been the last of her kind for even then she was unique. At home we had Girls or Edith Pearl Burrows but you'd never call them a Cook. A Cook came from literature.

Amy could not cook and did not profess to. She was a

literary female which in those days was considered enough. Writers did not get interviewed in the press about their domestic talents, they were just writers, good, bad or indifferent, and were expected to be covered with ink, with a dreamy look in the eye. But Launce was a gourmet and when Sue was out he went to the kitchen and made exciting dishes. At Gordon you didn't go Up the Road, or Up the Junction or even Up the Shops; you went to The Village, with a basket and a dog and at weekends Uncle Launce came too, in tweeds, with a stick. I found this exotic. My father never went to buy food.

"Tirra-lirra,

By the river,

Sang Sir Lancelot!" Uncle Launce would sing as he cooked. "That fellow must have been a terrible sissy."

"Terrible!" Amy would say, giggling. "Fancy anyone singing *Tirra-lirra!*"; but sometimes when we had been sent to bed in the four-poster we would hear our uncle singing in a quite different voice, while Dimsie played. The beauty of Stevenson's "Requiem" roughened my skin, but it was so sad, so *sad.*

Amy did not sing; except when she did the Sextette from *Lucia,* taking all six parts herself.

Every Sunday this uncle and aunt were At Home and people sat on the square veranda and looked at The Wilderness and ate gem scones and talked. Later they had cold chicken and claret at the round shining purple-mahogany dining table or by the sittingroom log-fire that smelt so delicious.

Among the artists and writers there were usually some of our aunt's female friends from the National Council of Women, in which she was active; dedicated pioneers fighting for better conditions, for higher standards in health, education, child welfare, employment; for international peace. To us they were only elderly ladies who never stopped talking, some of whose names offered scope ... Mrs Muscio (Mrs Moustachio); Mrs Preston Stanley (Mrs Pressed-on Badly); Miss Portia

Geach (Miss Portia Screech); Mrs Pankhurst Walsh (Mrs Spankhurst Walsh). When they had plain names like Rose Scott and Ruby Board we had to content ourselves with imitating their speech.

Apart from the militant women, whom we found rather formidable, there were more approachable ladies . . . Dora Wilcox, a sad poetess in a cloak with a sad husband called William Moore; Gladys Owen, a lively painter with dangling earrings and plaits round her ears like Chelsea buns, who married another Mr Moore called John D.; and a bright dark young woman whom Amy loved and who made us laugh, called Connie Stephens. She was a journalist and the daughter of A. G. Stephens of the *Bulletin*, who had been a great friend of our Aunt Louise. This Connie, who became Mrs Robertson, one day distressed and baffled me by saying she had *printer's ink in her veins*.

Sometimes there were shy students of Launce's, gauche clever young men, plain earnest bespectacled young women who doted on the Professor and performed little chores for Amy.

In general, the men seemed rather quieter than the women. Mr Minns, Mr Ure Smith, Lionel Lindsay were artists; Godfrey Smith played the piano; John D. Moore was an architect, Mr Fletcher was Editor of the *Herald* and Felix Barton had an unconventional school called Turramurra College where the boys seemed to do as they liked.

There were also professors who lived round about: Professor Edgeworth David, with a kind, beautiful face; Professor (History) Wood; Professor (Japan) Sadler, with a fascinating Japanese wife; Professor Waterhouse, who was making a marvellous garden which Amy privately disapproved of, being all for wild flowers unadorned; and our favourite, Professor (Greek) Woodhouse.

Plump, pink-faced, with white walrus moustache and slightly pop-eyes, a soft voice and enchanting giggle, his heart and most of his mind were in Ancient Greece. If we were said to talk of Abraham and Isaac as though they lived next door, the same could be said of him and the people of Homer.

We never thought of him as a distinguished scholar. We loved him for his looks, his gentleness, his funniness, his child's heart. When he talked of Greece I could see and smell it, arid, bare, full of fine white dust, the scent of wild thyme and antiquity.

"Tell us about the donkey, Professor Woodhouse."

He would take a breath, wipe the undersides of his moustaches, rest his hands on his knees, bend his elbows out and say obligingly in his mild precise voice, "And then there came forth from the village an old old man, born in the time of Homer, and with him a very young, very frail youth. And they said, 'We have a donkey which you may have to ride over the mountains', and I thanked them, for I was grateful. Then they brought forth the donkey! With such pride! Ah me! For it was so *old*! It too had been born in the time of Homer. It was the father of *all* donkeys, and so small, so thin, so fragile I knew it would not even carry me out of the village, let alone over the mountains, for I am not a lightweight!" and he would pat his portly stomach and shake with amusement.

Yet his gentleness was not without flavour.

"I see so-and-so has his knighthood at last!" said one of the Intellectuals rather sourly. There was a protesting chorus.

"The whole thing is such a *farce* now, one wouldn't *want* a knighthood . . . ."

"It's far more distinguished NOT to be in the Birthday Honours . . . ."

"I should feel I had lost my self-respect if I accepted a knighthood."

But Professor Woodhouse said wistfully, "If I thought it would get me a knighthood, I would gladly crawl on my stomach from the university to Circular Quay."

We were not invited to stay on for the chicken and claret suppers until we were growing up but while still very young were often included in the Harrison's house-parties. In the summer vacations, when not conducting groups of students on expeditions or exploring the Australian countryside, Launce and Amy took a house by the sea, at Palm Beach or Austinmer.

At Palm Beach we stayed in Miss Garran's house, *Four Winds*, on Sunrise Hill. ("What an address!" said an ecstatic friend. *"Four Winds, Sunrise Hill, Palm Beach!"*) The people who came to stay were usually artists or writers or academics of some kind, most of them fodder for our private mockery. We saw many distinguished citizens in a somewhat unflattering light, for Culture and Intellect do not always look their best on the beach; nor did the swimming costumes of the Twenties help very much. We could not understand how the owners of these hairy legs, weedy torsoes, sagging bosoms, flabby thighs could so calmly, so *unapologetically* reveal them in public; nor, of course, could they swim.

The ladies went down to Bathe in towelling Opera Cloaks with ruched collars. Their legs were blue-white and mottled, their heads covered with mackintosh mob-caps. They wore rubber slippers called surf-shoes which they kept on in the water, because female grown-ups had hideous feet with crooked toes and bunions and carbuncular pus-coloured corns and thick yellow nails.

Some ladies had old two-piece costumes but the more daring wore navy-blue stockingette cylinders which neither concealed nor uplifted.

The men were even more grotesque, lily-white and repulsive. Like the women, they never stopped talking. On the bush track going down, on the sand, in the sea they continued their endless discussions in loud fruity voices . . . . "Who's going to get the Bosch Chair?" . . . "Wallace [Vice-Chancellor] was dumbfounded." . . . "Selle [Registrar] was furious." . . . "I'm doing my autobiography, Amy; who do you suggest as publisher?" The Zoological Expedition to Barrington Tops and Launce's work on the skink lizard . . . The Science Expedition to Western Australia with a special train, where Launce discovered two new frogs . . . "Afraid you've rather missed the

74

bus, my dear, with a book on China." . . . "Amy, what do you think of X?" (an ambitious political barrister) . . . "Terrible little bounder!" "Ada Holman's book on her trip abroad." . . . "Not enough TALKS on the ABC programmes." . . . "If you heard what Gladys Marks has to say about policemen censoring books." . . . "Marcel's called his book *Highway into Spain* . . . ."

Only our uncle and aunt escaped our censure. Majestic, tanned, in a one-piece with cut-outs under the armholes, Launce took us on his shoulders into the very deep water and taught us to shoot breakers while the others shrilled and floundered about in the shallows.

Though as a beach-girl Amy was rather a let-down we turned a blind eye because we loved her. When she emerged from her towelling cloak she revealed a small dumpy figure in black sateen, a long-sleeved Russian blouse gathered in to a belt, frilling out round the hips. Beneath were knee-length drawers from which black stockings descended. On her feet were sandshoes and on her head, over a mob-cap, a cotton handkerchief tied in front like an old Southern mammy.

In this outfit she immersed herself gingerly, vertically, in the shallows and with one toe on the bottom, keeping her head above water, made circling arm movements. This was called Bathing. (It rhymes with scathing.)

My mother, wearing a similar costume, swam the same way. She called it Dipping In and Dipping Out.

Since no one used protective make-up on the beach and the female Intellectuals despised feminine deceptions there were many raw noses, scarlet faces and salt-stiffened straw heads at dinner each night.

Life was simple. There were no cars. You walked down Sunrise Hill to the surf and up again; you slid down and toiled up the vertical bush-track of *Four Winds* to and from Gow's Store, on Pittwater, for supplies. There was no cinema, no radio. People made their own entertainments. At the end of the day the Harrisons' friends sat on the veranda and watched the sun set over Pittwater, still talking. I took the conversations home:

"Look at Laahn Island! How LIKE a laahn he is!"

"Isn't he *grand*! Look at his tail!"

At night the men camped on the veranda in rows of folding beds while the ladies, smelling of sunburn cream, slept inside. There was no electricity. By nine o'clock Palm Beach lay silent and dark.

10

Parties

EXCEPT for my mother, we were summer people at heart. Winter was struggled through and quickly put out of mind, was in fact never officially recognized, due to my parents' spartan regime, by any additional comforts or warming aids.

Heat, when you live in a cool house by the sea, means freedom, bare feet, licensed laziness. There was always the beach, the cold shower, iced drinks and cool frothy puddings. At night people hosed gardens, evoking the scent of water on dust, or sat on their balconies waiting for the Southerly. Disembodied voices came flat through the dark. The smoke of my father's cigar mingled with the scent of stock. Debussy, fragmentary, sounded from a distant window.

When, in heat waves, the upstairs bedrooms were hot, excitement countered fatigue. One lay in citronella-scented darkness or under a net perversely enjoying discomfort because it could overthrow authority. You could go downstairs at any hour and not be reproved if you said, "It's too hot to sleep." My mother, gasping for the Southerly, often stayed up all night at such times, making tea, hosing plants, limply stretched on the balcony chaise-longue. Cap over eyes, the one-eyed cat slumped on his chest, my father reclined in his armchair, prolonging his music far into the night.

To wander into the garden in your nightgown, even go out

77

to the road and sit on still-warm asphalt, feeling the dark hot air on face and arms was liberation. Up the hill from the beach came nocturnal swimmers, slowly, murmuring, pausing to rest, to turn and walk backwards, which was said to lessen the strain.

Sheet lightning flashed across the sky above the Heads. Outlined against stars, possums crept in the trees.

One sensed more than heard the movement; a sigh yet not a sigh; a distant awakening. The flaccid air became informed with life. A moist salt smell moved in from the sea. My mother rushed to shut windows against the wind she had been craving. In the study the one-eyed cat reared into a Delos-lion posture, yawning avidly. My father, ever-ready for action, removed his patent fly-screens from his windows and battened the ship down against the gale.

Sometimes it was a storm. Worse off than before, since now the heat was shut inside, you sweltered as thunder crashed. Trees writhed and creaked; the air was charged with electricity. Disturbed possums thumped and hissed in sudden sexual excitement.

On the front veranda my father and Sheila watched the storm playing on the water, marvellously unafraid of red-hot wires in the sky and shattering detonations. In panic, I put away scissors and knives which I believed would bring lightning into the house, pulled down blinds and cowered under the bedclothes, flayed by a primitive terror far beyond rational fear. Though I squeezed my lids tight, each vicious flash sent a lilac flare through my coverings, shocking my whole inner being. Lightning created a physical response so appalling I can only assume I must have left a previous life by this medium.

Till the age of six, this fear of storms could be tempered by my mother's presence. Though each tautened nerve was still seared I believed she could protect by holding my hand, evoking normality, stability, the consciousness of our house round us, shutting out elemental forces. But one night, suddenly, though windows were shut and curtains drawn, lights burning, knives and scissors concealed and my mother there by my bed, I knew. Not she nor the safe well-lit room, the familiar ritual or the house itself could protect me. No one, nothing could give security, from storms or any other disaster. I was alone. We were all alone, always, for ever.

It was shocking, yet full of a strange exhilaration. *Now*, I knew, *I'm on my own*!

Sometimes these violent storms turned to heavy noctural rains that soaked and seeped so that morning was full of un-antipodean softness. Those were days from the West of Scotland, from Exmoor, the Black Sea coast, any moist green northern land; days when the world began again, with a silky bay, limpid air, loaded trees dripping gently, reviving birds and a sea wide and clear and sighing, rather relieved that all was over. But more often the Southerlies passed on like noisy trains and heat returned next day with grinding locusts and the perverse delight of limp exhausted bodies.

There were other nights when we stayed late on the balcony watching the persimmon glow above Clontarf, the nightlong flare in the sky. Sometimes the fires reached Grotto Point and the whole headland raced into flames. Smells of charred wood, of smoke drifted over the water, the sound of crackling. The bay reflected saffron peninsulas.

"No one lives there," my parents would comfort us. "There are no houses or people." But what of the birds, the animals, the soft furry life of the bush? Where did they go when the fire burnt down to the rocks at the edge of the sea? When the morning sun glared down on blackened stumps and elephant-coloured earth I could not pretend not to know.

There were more subtle fears than fires and storms.

"The next war," my father would say dispassionately, as searchlights played across the Heads, "will be from the air. Man was never intended to fly. He will pay for his impudence by his own destruction."

His detachment was chilling. The next war. The end of the world; unreal but ominous. The blue-grey shafts were sinister, cold, like the rays of a dead sun; yet how beautiful as they soared like reaching arms, raking the sky, then paused and with a breath-taking sweep reeled and fell and sank into the sea.

During the war I wrote to my parents from London, suggesting they might retire from that balcony, for the duration at least. My mother replied: "Dad says he's been here for 35 years and he's not going to move for any damned Japs. Besides, we couldn't leave the view . . . ."

Both my parents loved giving parties; so, apart from their own adult gatherings, our life was studded with childish rorts and teenage dances.

My mother would suddenly cry, "Let's have a PARTY!!" and start searching for pencil and paper. "Who will we *ask*?"

Our response was so encouraging we would soon have eighty or ninety names and be squabbling about whose friends should have priority.

My mother would begin to simmer long before the date, rising to full boil as it approached. In the last week my father would come home each night with flags, awnings, paper lanterns, coloured lights, balloons, decorations, new gramophone records and, when we were very small, new slides for the Magic Lantern. Cursing and swearing, he climbed up trees to string fairy lights round the garden or wavered on ladders, hanging decorations and Chinese lanterns on the balcony or streamers across the diningroom. Hot acetylene smells and stenches of blistering paint would come from his study where the Magic Lantern was being tried out or the sounds of new waltzes and funny men, played over and over.

My mother, short-tempered and flustered, would make food lists and telephone tradesmen. Piles of bread, boxes of sausage rolls, hams, chickens, fruit and lettuce, iced cakes and chocolates—*Don't touch!*—would clot up the kitchen. Sheafs of ferns, hydrangeas and shasta daisies stood in buckets, awaiting arrangement. The ice-chest was stuffed with forbidden goodies and for twenty-four hours before the party we lived on sandwiches.

On the day of the party the ice-man brought extra ice wrapped in sacks. It was stood in basins where it melted and ran and made puddles all over the floor. Soon after breakfast our Aunt Lily Creagh would arrive to make the icecream. This was done, I do not know how, with custard, saltpetre and a wooden churn with a handle which she patiently turned for hours. The result was a yellowish liquid full of sharp ice-crystals, but it made our parties much sought-after. In later years icecream came ready-made in bulk containers packed round with saltpetre and covered with canvas. We felt more sophisticated and without doubt the icecream was better; yet an irreplaceable touch of excitement went with our Aunt Lily's wooden churn.

The day of the party was always hot.

In the kitchen my mother, an aunt or two and the current domestic sat among ravishing smells of hardboiled eggs, passion-fruit, pineapples, cucumber, cutting, chopping, squeezing, spreading, waving off flies, dabbing at predatory fingers. Outside the back door my father converted the back veranda into an Eastern bower. Flags enclosed the open sides, streamers criss-crossed the ceiling, the diningroom carpet, moved out for the dancing, was spread on the floor. The carpentry bench was transformed into an elegant buffet by Nan Tay's embroidered tablecloths and silver vases of ferns.

Parties meant a great deal of tidying up, of thrusting things into cupboards, out of sight, out of mind. The whole house was fair game . . . drawingroom for receiving, balcony and staircase for sitting out, my mother's room for the girls' coats, my father's den for those inevitable youths who wanted to talk of boats, the diningroom cleared out for dancing, the back veranda for supper. Though out of sight, our bedrooms were not immune, for people went upstairs to the lavatory.

By the time preparations were done we were all bad-tempered, but orders to lie down and have a rest were ignored for fear of missing excitement. We slid up and down in the diningroom, shrieking hysterically, treading boracic into the floor. When we came downstairs—far too early—in our new dresses, hectically flushed, appetites ruined by too much picking, ready to fight or weep at any moment, my mother would become Russian. Emerging from her room, her hand pressed to her forehead or clapped to her heart, she would cry despairingly, *"No one's coming!"*

She had done this all her life, our aunts told us, but it never failed to convince. Sheila's lip would tremble; I would go rigid with shock. Only John remained cheerful, thinking of all the party food. When people did start arriving—strange how always the plainest and fattest girls came first—my mother's cry would be, "There won't be enough to eat!" But this was less disastrous, since we felt we could safely ignore it.

My father, unconcerned whether they came or not, or whether there was enough to eat, would be absorbed in his self-chosen functions, operating the Magic Lantern or in later years standing by the gramophone, winding up, changing records. Now and then he would take a turn round the floor with me or a favourite small girl—always the prettiest and most animated—like Royalty bestowing patronage. He was, as my mother claimed, a beautiful dancer.

I longed to dance all the time. To me a party meant a new dress and myself in it, whirling endlessly round the floor with a romantic partner. But it never turned out like that, no matter how many the offers. It had been drilled into us that neither Sheila nor I could dance if other girls had no partners.

"You can NOT dance while so-and-so's sitting out!" my mother would say, recalling me from the floor with a stern glance. "You *must* look after your friends before you enjoy yourselves."

This was bad enough, since there was always someone sitting out—usually fat detested daughters of my mother's old school friends—but even worse was having to dance with them oneself. It was less the indignity of a female partner, which did not disturb me so much, as the feel of those fearful stomachs, pushing you round the room.

Under Chinese and Japanese lanterns people sat out on the balcony. Later—much later—they went into the garden. This was condemned as Fast. Amorous older cousins who enticed girls out there were reprimanded. Mothers known to my parents sat round the diningroom walls like dowagers and bore their daughters away before any young man could see them home. I don't know how any of us ever got married.

Left in an echoing ballroom among wilting ferns and balloons, with snowy foot-prints all over the house, we lay back exhausted and talked it over. Out in the kitchen hired women washed up and stacked plates. Close friends stayed the night to assist in post-mortems. Driven upstairs at last we talked the rest of the night away and slept most of the following day. This my mother called Sleeping your Sleep Out and prevented you looking Washed Out. She believed girls must be Fresh and have Lovely Complexions. Towards evening there would be a dash to the beach for a swim; then, dreamily, picking at scraps from the party and back to bed. Next day, at school, it was all gone over again, and so on, with decreasing excitement till not a shred for discussion was left; always, without fail, to be pronounced by my mother—her forecasts of doom forgotten —*The best one we ever had!*

I I

Poor Henry

BECAUSE of our Mack aunts and my father's tastes, writers were part of our background; but names heard too often, episodes told too many times lose their power. We were not much impressed by the literary figures our elders talked of unless outrageously colourful or eccentric.

Henry Lawson, now a national symbol engraved on bank notes, was at one time confused in my mind with my uncle Fred whom we saw infrequently. Both lived at Manly, both had sad dark eyes and drooping moustaches, both were objects of pity, both had vague marital troubles, both had a failing, though Fred's was temporary and Henry's chronic; and both were referred to as *Poor*.

Poor Fred had rather a high voice and was given to mournful songs. Pounding a jangling piano, against a background of drear winds and monotonous surf, he would moan, "Goodbye Fare Thee Well", and "Nita, Juanita, Ask thy soul if we should part". Or he would try to be gay and sing a Darkeytype song called "The Ring-tailed Coon", while we stood stiffly, hot with discomfort, longing to escape. We viewed him uneasily, never knowing when he might call our friends Little Damsels or come out with some sick-making antique gallantry that would evoke scorn among our contemporaries for days.

Hapless adults inspire embarrassment more than compassion

in the heartless young. Fred and Henry with their doggy eyes and moustaches gave one the creeps.

Poor Henry's name was mainly associated with financial distress: ". . . On the quay . . . no money for ferry . . . Poor Henry!" "Poor Henry in George Street . . . he touched me . . ." "Poor Henry . . . no lunch, so I gave him . . ."

"Poor Henry," our Aunt Amy would say. "How often I've given him the price of a drink."

"I've often helped him across the street," said Louise, in one of her books.

"Was he lame?"

"No. Squiffy. They drink, you know, Australian poets."

If you asked why Poor Henry was always hard up my mother and aunts would be evasive.

"Because . . . because he's a Poor Simple Fellow. A Nice Amiable Kindly Fellow with a Weakness."

"What sort of weakness?"

"He's a boozer," my father would say drily.

"Dear, you shouldn't TELL them things like that," my mother would say, as though Henry's boozing were all her fault. She avoided words like *drink* or *drunk*. People had Failings or Weaknesses or were Not Well.

"You can't get away from it, Dearie. The feller's a chronic boozer."

My Aunt Amy was inclined to say dismissingly, "He's just a Poor Unfortunate!"; but my mother, who found excuses for people, would point out that Henry was deaf and had sad eyes. And when my father repeated, "He's a drunk!" would recite her creed: "Men—drink—when—they—DON'T—GET FED PROPERLY!"

I don't think my father had much time for Poor Henry, whose verse he described as *Terrible poor stuff*.

The story that most appealed to me, about this writer, was of a picnic on Middle Harbour, with George Rignold, the actor, my father and John le Gay Brereton, the poet. They set out in a very small boat on a very hot day with a great deal of beer which was so potent that eventually my father and the two poets threw off their clothes and dived overboard among the sharks. George Rignold, with his flair for theatre, stood on a rock wearing straw hat and boots and declaimed Mark Anthony's oration, before diving, fully dressed, into the harbour.

My parents and aunts were very fond of John le Gay Brereton who was lovable, sunburnt, untidy and as eccentric in his own way as my father. He was a health crank and wore special shirts designed by himself with holes for breathing, so my father said. He also practised nudism and vegetarianism whenever possible and when he came to stay brought his own food, which he carried in a tin pannikin. Vegetarians, my father explained, lived on sawdust and woodshavings.

When my mother remonstrated about the sawdust he would describe a night camping out in a boatshed at Botany Bay. While he and his fellow lawyer, Jim Pickburn, enjoyed salthorse and beer, Jack Brereton ate sawdust rissoles. My father tasted one. He said it contained bits of razor-blade and was held together with office paste.

"You children get the most *peculiar* information from your father," our Aunt Amy would say, half-amused, half-disapproving. It was true. Banjo Paterson, for instance, who now appears on postage stamps, was just a lawyer who wrote verse, a laconic cove, amusing but not much of a poet. Just a balladist; mainly memorable for a remark he made at the Boer War, where he went as war correspondent. Up in the front line the flies were terrible, clouds darkening the air so you could hardly see. When Banjo Paterson asked how the soldiers endured them, he was told, "They're not flies. They're bullets!"

And Christopher Brennan, now acclaimed a giant, was merely one of my father's contemporaries who had been in his year doing Arts; a queer cove, moody, eccentric. You never knew where you were with him. Independent, brilliant, charming if he felt like it and had a chance to hold the floor, but unpredictable. A fine scholar, a fine poet, a boozer. He used to bring a bag of stones into lectures and if he became bored or did not care for the lecturer would roll them down the aisle, slowly, one by one, at long intervals.

Neither Brennan's achievements in poetry and scholarship nor even his tragic decline could ever surpass in my mind that youthful protest against boredom.

Though Lionel Lindsay frequented my Aunt Amy's parties his brother Norman was not of the company and we knew him only as the wonderful author of *The Magic Pudding* and *Saturdee*. Rather later, when he was under a cloud with the righteous, I was startled and thrilled to be invited to visit him. A friend had shown him some verse I had written and he was amused.

I felt it best not to tell my mother where I was going. Climbing the grimy stairs to the studio in Bridge Street I thought uneasily of my father, just up the road in Union House.

Breathless with nerves, stairs and excitement, I knocked on the studio door, but the moment it opened I found myself laughing. A gay, small, slim, familiar figure, with Julius Caesar fringe and grubby old cardigan, out at the elbows, stood offering a frail, warm hand; familiar yet different, for no photograph had prepared me for the brilliance, the bubbling vitality. No picture showed the delicate bird-bones, the silky skin, the luminous, sea-coloured eyes.

At once, he began talking. He perched, winding his legs, on a high stool. He talked quickly and laughed a great deal. His lips were red and rather moist; his remarkable eyes full of sparkling humour. He regarded me quizzically, just like my dear Uncle Sid. I felt completely at home.

The studio seemed rather dark for painting, I think the lights were on. Perhaps curtains were drawn; there was a general effect of heavy hangings and drapes. Rich antique costumes of velvet and satin, with pearls and embroidered stomachers were piled up or hung on a lay-figure, and canvases were stacked about. The sink draining-board was littered with unwashed plates and cups, opened jam tins and numerous egg-shells. There was a good deal of dust and the kind of confusion which, I knew from my reading, belonged to the Left Bank of Paris.

"I'll make you some tea," said Norman Lindsay. "I'm the only one who knows how to make tea. I have my own method." The words were familiar. "Are you hungry? How about an egg? Let's have a boiled egg."

It was three o'clock and no time for eggs but I would have eaten anything he suggested. He skipped and hopped and jerked about at the sink, growing rather snappy when I offered to wash up. There was no salt for the egg and the tea was on a par with my father's, but the company compensated. Like my mother, though with different results, he was a parson's child.

"The little boy with the velvet suit in *Saturdee* . . . My God, my mother dressed me like that. She wanted a girl! Ha ha. It's a wonder I didn't grow up a homosexual. Have some more tea. *Flaxen curls*! Little Lord Fauntleroy. Ha ha. You'd be too young to remember. How's your egg? Have another?"

At my request he showed me some paintings, pointing out that the wowsers wouldn't care for them. I agreed, like a well-seasoned libertine, that wowsers were hopeless; but now he was talking of music, of Uncle Wattlebury, of ships. It was hard to keep up; and all the time he skipped and frisked and danced or twined his legs round his stool.

Nor was he only funny and fascinating; he was kind. He gave advice about my verses and made suggestions. Emerging at last, in a daze, I walked straight into my father, on his cane-swinging way down Bridge Street to the Quay.

He raised his cane in the usual salute and asked where I had been.

"I've been to see Norman Lindsay!" I said defiantly. *"In his studio!"*

My father gave a short amused laugh. I could see he was not

concerned for my virtue.

"Clever cove," he said. "Did he show you his model ships?" Then, marching on, "Best children's books ever written, *Magic Pudding* and *Saturdee*."

Though unimpressed in earlier years by individuals, I was stirred by the *idea* of writers, particularly in retrospect. When my parents and aunts talked, as they often did, of the old days of literary Sydney they made it sound like the Left Bank, a world of freedom and poverty, youthful ideals, literature, music and art. Their reminiscences created a sense of excitement and wild romance, of everything being new. Everyone was young and a genius, every work a masterpiece in that *belle époque*. To have a story accepted was wonderful; to publish a book quite stupendous, especially if you were a pretty young woman. Our aunt Louise was part of those days, when Henry Lawson and Banjo Paterson were publishing their first books and writers were being encouraged to write by J. F. Archibald and A. G. Stephens at the *Bulletin*, by George Robertson at Angus & Robertson and Lord Beauchamp at Government House.

It did not matter that I confused Sydney with Paris, real writers with fictitious characters, it was all *la vie de Bohême*. Writers, romantically, were eccentric, unreliable, often drunk, always hard up, lived in garrets and starved because they would not prostitute their art. Male writers were largely unwashed, stayed up all night, and if they had female companions or children you could bet they were not legal. Women writers wore very queer clothes and coiffures, were sternly blue-stocking in pince-nez or soulful with hair in a cloud; but all were people apart, infinitely preferable and superior to the most worthy businessmen or suburban housewives.

It was true that some male writers turned respectable, that the females sometimes retired to comfortable matrimony. I had met such lady writers at my Aunt Amy's, had seen their tasteful houses with antiques and jonquils in phallic vases and limp leatherbound Poets with William Morris covers in gold. Drypoints and etchings hung on their pale distempered walls. They were very cultured, travelled in Port Line ships, knew London as intimately as Sydney. As time passed they grew stout and grey-haired and rather deaf and faintly moustached and given to cloaks made of Middle East textiles and Benares beaten-silver shawls; but none of this could entirely kill the romance of their pasts, the lingering aura of Bohemia, the glamour of having had their books *published*.

Being published crowned your life, like going to Mecca.

One day, as a treat, my Aunt Amy took me to Angus and Robertson to see Mr Robertson. After meeting this historic personage, surprisingly mild and elderly, I was told to wait outside while she discussed her business. Excited by the smell of new books, I studied the rows of sepia photographs on the wall: gentlemen with high collars pushing up their chins, pince-nez, moustaches, hair smarmed down from a centre parting and challenging manly expressions. The ladies had fluffed-out side pieces, bandeaux or hats, ecstatic expressions and hints of camisoles. Some of them were familiar. My Aunt Amy was there, in a highwayman tricorne and redingote, looking keenly out from her standing-up collar, and Louise, head thrown back, proud, theatrical, wildly cosmopolitan in a black Cossack hat and negligent furs, the Lady Authoress to the last sealskin whisker.

When Amy rejoined me I said in excitement, "That's you!"

"Yes." Simpering. "That's me!"

"And Aunty Louie!"

"Yes, that's Louie."

"Who's that?" a face with pince-nez I had often seen at her house.

"That's Mary. Mary Gilmore. And that's Will Ogilvie . . . a *great* friend of ours when we were young. A Scottish poet. He spent his last night in Australia in our house, before he went back to England . . . long before you were born. . . ."

She talked on . . . Victor Daley, Bertram Stevens, dear Rod

Quinn, Poor Henry . . . but I wasn't listening. I stared at the sepia faces, groping. I had always thought of these people as ancient, as boring friends of my elders; now I suddenly saw them in focus. They were still antique but different, more impressive, authoritative. Was it because they were tidied up, with their hair brushed, wearing their best clothes? Or because they had reached the distinction of hanging here in this shrine where books were published?

". . . our Australian writers!" said my aunt in a proud educational voice. "And *one* of these days"—it was the fairy doll from the top of the tree—"if you work hard and learn to *spell* properly, your picture might be here too. You might be a writer!"

12

The Scarlet Letter

To universal astonishment, soon after I left Killarney, my nose, which my father described as "caught in the door", turned into a Creagh nose, even more highly esteemed than straight teeth. This almost overshadowed the excitement of leaving kindergarten for a big school.

My mother and her sisters went to the Sydney Girls High School; but times had changed, Mrs Garvan, the great headmistress, had retired, the High School was not what it was. Since the Macks were Methodists and my father nothing orthodox I do not know why we were finally sent to Church of England schools. Perhaps because they were handy, for my parents would never have entertained thoughts of boarding-school.

In turn, Sheila and I graduated from cutting-out and pasting-in, at Killarney, to black stockings and hair in two plaits, to morning prayers, divinity three times a week and a thorough grounding in early church history and prayer-book ritual. This came in very handy later when I lived in an English rectory. We also learnt to draw maps of St Paul's missionary journeys, to play tennis and netball, to sing *Orf-yoos, with his loot, His loo-hoot made trees . . .* and *Philomel with melodeee, Sing in our sweet lullabyyyy.* School spirit, which we were expected to display, was fostered by such measures as the

Harrow song, "Forty Years On". We liked the mournfully militant air and did not find it strange that Australian schoolgirls should chorus, *"Till the field rings again and again, With the tramp of the twenty-two men."*

The year after I left Killarney John moved on to a prep school with a headmaster known as Tibbie. Here he learnt the catechism, how to play cricket and football and call boys by their surnames. He was also put in the choir and sang "Hear my Prayer" in such an angel's voice that ladies wept and said he was better than Master Ernest Lough.

Our real education was received at home; yet though liberal in some ways it was really very lopsided. We lived in an ivory tower, aware of certain events in the great world, out of touch with others.

Melba, Pavlova, Heifetz, Paderewski, Kreisler, Chaliapin . . . we saw and heard them all, no matter how much went over our heads; but less agreeable happenings registered only when they personally concerned ourselves: the Japanese earthquake because we had relations there; the *Greycliffe-Tahiti* collision because my father acted for the Union Steamship company in the court case that followed; the Depression because some of our friends had to leave school and get jobs; the dismissal of the N.S.W. premier J. T. Lang by the Governor, Sir Philip Game, because we had been told he would RUIN my father.

History and geography were matters of personal association. What was Russia? Warmhearted people in brightcoloured clothes, like my wooden *matrioshka*, peasants whirling round in boots and *rubashkas, droshkis* chased by wolves across snow, tea from samovars like the one at Jemima's, sad songs like "The Red Sarafan" which we learnt at home or dark beautiful music that made you nostalgic for a country you had never seen. And a sinister memory, far far back, a night on the balcony when, forgotten, I crouched in the shadows and heard the grown-ups talk in shocked subdued voices. The Tsar and his family . . . killed by the Bolsheviks . . . butchered in cold blood.

What were Bolsheviks?

"Your Uncle Gus and his family," Jemima would tell us, "had to flee during the Russian Revolution. Everything left behind. Just the clothes they stood up in. Your little cousin Brian was born in the Military Hospital at Vladivostok . . . ."

"Your Uncle Gus *loves* the Russians; but *Those Bolsheviks!* They summoned him to the Tribunal. He was very brave. He knew it was no good trying to defend himself so he didn't take even a pistol. Just his little cane. Quite calm, he went and faced them!"

"And his Russian friends saved him! He had been making complaints to the Government, writing to the papers, trying to improve the terrible conditions of the men who worked in the gold mine where he was in charge. Your Uncle Gus is a mining engineer and he is a very *kind* man . . . he could not bear to see the way the poor Russians had to work and live. So when The Bolsheviks arrested him his friends produced all the evidence of what he had been trying to do for the poor Russians and the Tribunal gave him twenty-four hours to get out of the country! So you see his life was saved because he was a good and kind man . . . ."

Russian *moujiks* and *babushkas*, Japanese in umbrella hats and *mompei*, Italian *contadine* in straw hats, Mexicans in *serapes*, Indians in saris, Mesopotamians in nightshirts . . . in some way they all belonged to our family because our relations had made them part of our lives; the whole world was one family, waiting impatiently till one was old enough to go and meet it oneself.

Compared to the eager way modern parents participate in their children's education, ours were strangely vague. They never went to school meetings or functions, except breaking-ups when we were getting prizes. My father had stipulated that we learn Latin, music, history and literature but was offhand about the rest. My mother, pestered in secret, agreed to one giving up maths, which then had to be taken up again in a hurry when one wanted to matriculate.

"The Macks could never do maths," she would say rather complacently. It was a family tradition. When Sheila married a mathematician (a Cambridge Wrangler) our Aunt Alice marvelled: "Fancy Sheila marrying a man who can do *sums!*"

Though my father was paying for us to go to school I think he had more confidence in his own methods of education. Ever since I can remember he had been prone to share with us whatever he was reading at meals . . . Voltaire, Roman Law, Shakespeare, Dr Johnson, Dickens or Cicero. He believed we should be exposed to the best from the start and had little patience with Tales Retold for the Young. We were allowed the run of his library, for he held that what was Too Old for us would pass over our heads. I took advantage of this to display at school an illustrated edition of *Mademoiselle de Maupin*.

"Oooh!" said the Lower Fourth happily, snatching from each other. "Your father has Awful books."

As soon as we could read easily, intensive treatment began. Every third Friday night my father brought home three literary classics of some kind, one for each of us. By the end of the third week we had to have read and be able to answer questions on all three books. We then got another three.

It was easy if you got books like *Trilby* or *Tom Sawyer*, but some, though fascinating, were immense—like *The Man in the Iron Mask*, while others, such as *The Scarlet Letter*, were plain dull.

All one hot Saturday afternoon I lay on the hall floor, drowsy from swimming and sun, struggling with this dreary tale. I could not understand what it was all about, why such a fuss was being made about the letter *A*, what Hester Prynne had *done*. I plodded on, wondering how I should give an account of such an inexplicable story and how soon I could lay hands on Sheila's *Three Musketeers*.

"You're *poring* over that book!" said Aunty Amy, who was visiting. "Sit up straight. What are you reading?"

I showed her. "It's called *The Scarlet Letter*," I said apathetically.

To my surprise she snatched.

"Where did you get that book?"

"Dad gave it to me."

"Your *father*?"

Astonished at her reaction, I thankfully watched her carry the book away and might have lost interest but for a conversation overhead.

"Really Billy! At that age! What can you be thinking of?"

"What's age got to do with it? She reads perfectly well."

"That's just what I mean. Most unsuitable. *At her age.*"

"It's a good book. They've got to learn to tell good work from bad. What she doesn't understand won't hurt her."

Amy gave her exasperated snort.

"There are plenty of examples of good writing without giving your children books on *that subject.*"

What subject? What had I missed? It was clear from her tone that it was of the Run-upstairs-Nancy-and-find-my-glasses category; that I must get the book back.

At dinner that night I asked, "Where's my book?"

My mother looked innocent.

"What book?"

"My book I was reading that Dad gave me that Aunty Amy took."

"Oh," said my mother vaguely. "She probably left it in the drawingroom."

"It's not in the drawingroom," I began to wail. "It's not anywhere. She took it. She's pinched it!"

My mother said falsely, "You must have mislaid it. It's about somewhere. Aunty Amy wouldn't take it away. She has all the books she wants."

"Dad—" I said, but my mother contorted her face in the seizure that meant NOT IN FRONT OF THE CHILDREN. Cravenly he said, "I've got you a better one. That's pretty dull stuff."

Outraged at his cowardice I said no more, but after dinner went to my mother's room and thrust my hand under her mattress. This was where she hid books considered Unwholesome or Too Old. There was no *Scarlet Letter*. It must be so frightful, so vile it had been destroyed.

Consumed with curiosity, I searched for days—our house, Jemima's, the school library—determined to find out what *that subject* was. I found the book but that subject eluded me. *The Scarlet Letter* still went over my head, was still as boring and incomprehensible as before.

Though my father never censored our reading my mother occasionally made an effort to protect our minds.

"I will not have you reading that TRASH!" she would say, bearing off *Iron Ned Kelly and his Gang*. This sort of thing caused no protest. It was only a matter of waiting till she went out, of fetching the banned book from under her mattress, returning it before she came back.

We were introduced to bad literature as well as good, with ridicule for protection and guidance. My father's dry caustic wit was far more potent than any strictures or arguments that might have roused youthful defiance. By the time he had finished with an offending work it could never again be taken seriously.

His usual form of attack was to read aloud from the chosen book, in a sonorous declamatory manner. A favourite was called *A Tangled Garden*, which he claimed was the world's worst novel. It began:

"Lorna, will you marry me?" and after describing the speaker's pale face and soft drooping moustache, "A *keen* observer," my father would read with gusto, "would have considered Denis Ackroyd's face *admirably* suited to express the *fire* and *passion* of love!"

Our enjoyment of such works was increased by Sheila's artistic interpretations. Whatever book she was reading she drew as she went, in the margins, on odd scraps of paper, phrases, incidents, characters that appealed to her. Her drawings were witty, succinct and rather bawdy. Beneath her diffident manner was a roystering spirit her elders did not suspect.

This found its happiest expression in illustrating the Bible and Pepys' diary.

Both she and John drew as they breathed, ate, sang, as a natural necessity, putting no value on what they created; but I couldn't draw. I had to describe, so I stared, feeling for words. Though enjoyment of all kinds of people had been fed to us with our mother's milk and fostered constantly by both parents, illogically and unfairly I was always reproved for staring.

It was hard not to, there was so much to see ... the genteel Bod at the next table, index knuckle pressed under chin, pondering in arch hesitation—*Quite a meal, isn't it*! Gay, non-chalant, yet the greedy glint in the eye, the voice quivering with private eagerness. Then the angry whisper:

"Nancy, don't stare!"

And those male morning faces, in trams, glimpsed behind newspapers, the grape-bloom of shaving soap on mauvish complexions, eyes not quite open, not entirely divorced from sleep, not yet clicked back into day faces. Why did unknown men at that hour sometimes have a curious repulsive intimacy; still half-revealing off-guard nocturnal beings? But always as you groped and pondered, the whisper:

"Nancy, don't stare!"

Don't stare! Don't listen! How did they expect you to learn? Nan Tay's delicious monologues on internal female complaints (*Something Inward*) always began, "*This* one [Sheila] can stay. I know *she* won't repeat. The *Other* [Nancy] is All Ears." Then my mother would ask me to just run upstairs and get some absurd trifle; and if I hung round the closed door I was always caught. It was specially enraging that Sheila, the privil-eged, seemed unaware of her good fortune and had little interest in what was denied me.

Having ensured we could swim, lash and lace sails to spars, read the weather signals from the flags on Garden Island, sing sea shanties, play the piano and consume a literary classic a week, my father turned his attention to perfecting our musical ear. Prizes were offered for whistling a given Bach fugue, suite or concerto without mistake. Practice and auditions took place under the shower, my father listening keenly outside, periodically thumping the door to point out errors. I can still whistle most of the Brandenburgs, parts of French and English Suites and a number of fugues without missing a note.

Outside the bathroom we never knew when our parents would pounce, musically. The only time to play the piano in peace was when they were out.

"No no no no NO! Not like THAT!" my mother would cry, rushing in from the kitchen to push you away, putting her cooking spoon down on the keys; while my father would appear more quietly but no less critically at the drawingroom door, directing, beating time with head, hand and foot. If you happened to be singing Mozart you could expect them both together, my father to attend to the musical score, my mother to correct your Italian.

Mozart ran like a bright thread all through our singing life in that house: *Voi che sapete, Batti batti, Vedrai carino, Porgi amor, Dove sono, La ci darem, Deh vieni non tardar, Deh vieni all finestra* . . . Don Giovanni, Leporello, Figaro, Zerlina, Susanna, Cherubino all singing their heads off together. But it was not only Mozart and since we were each so absorbed in our own music that we were deaf to others, no matter how close, there were interesting combinations—my mother out in the kitchen singing a Neapolitan *canzonetta*, Sheila upstairs carolling *Im Wunderschönen Monat Mai*, John in the shower practising *Ombra Mai Fu*, Nancy at the piano trying out *Bist du bei Mir*, my father and the one-eyed cat enjoying the Beethoven Violin concerto.

The last movement of this concerto had been hopelessly ruined for us by Professor Woodhouse.

"Have you ever noticed, in Beethoven's Violin Concerto," he said one day in the midst of a classy musical conversation, "in the scherzo of the last movement?" and beating time with his soft hands he sang,

"Papa's home early, papa's home early,
Tra la, *tra* la, *tralla, tipputy-ta.*
Papa's home early, Papa's home early,
Tra la, *tra* la, *tra la la la la la la . . .*

"And then he goes on, as it were, to develop the theme in the form of a question . . .

Papa's home early?
Papa's home early?
Early? early? EARLY?

Oh, earlier earlier earl . . . ."

13

Carpentry

DESPITE his love for the arts my father was a man of rather austere tastes and frugal habits. He seemed unaware of certain luxuries, comforts, even household needs that most people take for granted when they can afford them. The place could fall down round your ears and he would not notice, so long as he had a book to read or music to listen to. His secretary always maintained he should have been a Chinese philosopher, so indifferent was he to money, so averse to sending in bills. When he died it was found he had never claimed thousands of pounds owed as loans, debts or guarantees of some sort.

Geographically placed in, but not of prosperous suburbia, we lived so stringently in some ways that we did not know our father was a man of substance and took it for granted that we were rather hard-up. Our parents did not participate in Society, they ridiculed display and pretentiousness and seemed to despise worldly success. Since neither had any respect for money —my father because he'd always had it, my mother because she'd never had any—we grew up unaware that special reverence was due to those richer than oneself.

Our parents' standards of acceptance were individual. Beyond the pale to my father were those who stood up in a boat, wore shoes in a boat, called a boat It, who sought publicity or indulged in self-advertisement. To my mother, outcasts included people who looked as though they never had a cold shower, slept with windows shut, who said *Pleased to meet you* or *Beg Yours,* who kept pubs or shops, and a mysterious form of life known as *parvenu.*

As John grew up he became very critical of my mother's distinctions.

"Bloody snobbery," he would rumble when she commented on friends he brought home from the boatshed. "Just because he doesn't go to the university!"

"It's nothing of the sort! He's not interested in any of the things you like. And he's so *rough.*"

"He's good in a boat. And some of the blokes at school are rough as bags but of course they're all right because they wear straw hats. Just because poor old Hec didn't go to Shore you sling off at him. Well, he's coming to dinner! I've asked him and he's coming!"

He came. A good ten years older than John, he thumped the table and abused The Professional Classes as he wolfed down the fruits of my father's ill-gotten gains.

My father, after listening quizzically to the tirade, retired without comment.

"What can you have in common with a man like that?" my mother moaned helplessly, fatally. "A carpenter!"

John grew very red in the face. His anger was slow but alarming.

"Jesus was a carpenter!" he bellowed. "I suppose He'd be good enough to come to dinner?"

Jesus apart, carpentry was accepted, perforce, in our house.

The Creaghs were great ones for fine handwork and fine equipment for doing it with. My grandfather Patrick, who learnt cabinet-making as a hobby, had a workshop fitted with bench and lathe and cases of beautiful tools.

They lay in shaped recesses in sweet-scented sandalwood boxes, delicate chisels and saws like surgical instruments, for wood carving and fretwork, as exquisite, complicated and comprehensive as the Creagh women's apparatus for sewing.

My father inherited the tools but not the skill, though my mother believed him an accomplished carpenter. With his complete disrespect for old or beautiful furniture he hammered nails into ancient mahogany, hacked at walnut, carved his way through endless cedar. Hot soldering-irons, saws, files scarred the surface of mellow tables, patent hinges and flaps were added to chests-of-drawers, blocks and tackle applied wherever space permitted. The inventor's frenzy was not confined to his study; the whole house was fair game. Gates and cupboards were weighted with flat-irons connected with wheels and wires, cat-and-dog-exits cut in doors, even the meat-safe, in the days before fridges, had a patent closer which snapped your fingers with vicious efficiency. My mother never dared express a wish for any new piece of furniture. Mention of a dumb-waiter produced a table mounted on six-inch rubber-tyred wheels, with battens, as for a rough sea, hammered round the sides. Reading lamps blossomed from lengths of metal piping.

Any form of domestic appliance or furnishing was regarded as a challenge. Even mousetraps could be improved. The simple spring type that effectively killed was replaced by a construction with a trap door that fell like a guillotine and imprisoned the mouse alive. This must then be disposed of next morning, to my mother's horrified shrieks and our wails and pleas for its life. A superior model was then devised with a high tower, a ramp, a springboard and a tin of water. The mouse ran in for the cheese, the trapdoor dropped, the mouse ran up the ramp to the top of the tower and dived off the springboard into the water where, theoretically, it drowned.

Though this gruesome, cumbersome and enormous toy was devised from my father's own inspired brain, there is a very similar model in the Tanunda Museum, used by early German settlers in the Barossa Valley of South Australia.

Carpentry took place in winter, on Sundays, sometimes far into the night. Brought up as a parson's daughter, my mother must have been shattered by first contact with a Creagh Sunday. Not only was there no church, no midday meal, no normal clothing, there was complete disregard of time. During the week my father was a model of circumspection; at weekends he demanded freedom.

In the early days she tried persuasion.

"How can I keep a servant?" she would plead. "Sunday is the girl's afternoon off. She wants to go out. She can't wash up till you've had your lunch. It's nearly three o'clock!" Later, she succumbed to his majestic indifference. We ate our lunch and left his food out. Towards four o'clock, having tea in another part of the house, we would hear the crashes and bangs, the swearing, stamping and slamming of cupboard doors that meant father was feeding.

"It's only Dad getting lunch," we would explain to visitors.

Most of our friends enjoyed, even envied us this performance, though sometimes a more bourgeois type, insisting on carrying the tea-tray out to the kitchen, would return looking stunned. It was a witch's cavern out there. Cauldrons bubbled, smoke rose from toasters, cold joints were savagely hacked. If knives were not sharp enough they were taken out to the grindstone where the wheel rotated with water and sparks flying out while flames rose like lotus petals round saucepans abandoned upon the stove.

I think my mother was really despairingly proud of her husband's inventive gifts. To friends and relations she spoke of them as of a wilful but favorite child. Though she protested, she never made any real effort to prevent him overflowing the house with his creations and the fruits of his experiments.

Perhaps the worst, from her point of view, were the gramophones. The drawing room had always been her province, a pale cool room where she played and sang and entertained ladies with fruit-cake and sherry-wine from an elegant little decanter. When the first gramophone came it did not intrude, a mere box on a table. The next model, on legs, with a cabinet beneath for records, fitted modestly into a corner and when closed could be used for the Chinese vase and portraits of our Uncle Sid in his wig, our Aunt Louise in her sables.

This cabinet with its listening fox-terrier, its sapphire needle, gave endless delight and amusement. Tenors bellowed, sopranos soared, orchestras boomed, comedians prattled. We listened, convulsed, to "The German on the Telephone" (*Vot you dair? Vot you dair? Oh, you vot!*); "How Bill Adams Won the Battle of Waterloo" and "The Meanderings of Monty" (*The Near East is not so far as the Far East—on account of the distance*). The Prince of Wales himself spoke to us in a high cracked voice about Sthporthsmanship; and Madame Melba, far away in a fog, sang "Home Sweet Home."

We were perfectly satisfied and would have remained so but for my father's perfectionism. Though the best gramophone he could buy, it was not good enough. The tone could be improved, the quality of the orchestra enriched, the voices made more resonant. Slowly at first, then with full fervour, he began to experiment.

The engine was removed from the cabinet and taken into his study. When next we saw it it was encased in a strange horizontal box like a coffin, which also contained a long metal square-sided horn. As far as I can remember, the length of the horn was to improve the tone and I think it did; but he was not satisfied. A square-sided glass horn was next constructed and fitted into the box. It was soon discarded and the metal replaced, but with the addition of sand. This was to be blown upon the walls of the horn, first prepared with wet paint, and when in action the grains would vibrate and increase resonance.

We were sent to the beach with buckets for the finest possible sand. It was carefully sifted of all impurities and blown on the sticky wet horn.

This was a great improvement and for a while it seemed there might be peace; but soon a new model appeared with a plywood horn. There were also cylindrical and oval horns, and the shape of the case varied . . . a sarcophagus, an aeroplane, a sea-chest or a mere egg-crate. Sometimes the horn was enclosed in the box, sometimes outside, like a monster loud-hailer.

Though my father was happy and fully absorbed we were disgruntled. For one reason, he did his tone-testing at night, playing a phrase over and over until you felt you could scream. A Bach fugue, a Beethoven quartet would begin, to be ruthlessly cut short and started again; Chaliapin would boom the same line, Galli-Curci trill the same notes over and over. When two different parts of the record were tested, the effect was even more exasperating.

> *The silver swan, who living had no note,*
> *When death appro . . .*
> *. . . all joys, Oh Death come clo . . .*
> *The silver swan, who living had etc. . . .*
> *. . . all joys, Oh Death come clo . . . etc.*

"I am sick of the sound of that gramophone," my mother would mutter behind her husband's back, and she would repair to a bed on the front veranda where she could not hear. Since my bedroom was directly above the experimental laboratory I received in full measure every unfinished note, every interrupted phrase so that I too had to move my mattress out to my roofless balcony where possums trod on my face and dew drenched me at dawn.

When we complained that we now had no gramophone, since it was always kept in the study, the sarcophagus, aeroplane, sea-chest, egg-crate, in turn, were brought into the drawingroom where, on a specially constructed coffin-rest, they remained. My mother was now worse off than ever. She had to look at the monstrosities but could not use them, since they were permanently in the experimental stage.

Though this restriction annoyed us, we children and our friends delighted in the physical forms of father's inventions and keenly awaited each new variation. These might have continued for ever, had not improved electrical recordings come in.

Radio entered our lives with less disturbance.

For some time my father had been enclosed in his lair, now a model for Heath Robinson, in absolute silence, except for occasional bursts of profanity. We knew nothing. No questions were permitted. It was to be a Surprise. Then one day we were summoned.

Our father was sitting at a table wearing earphones—the first I had ever seen. They were rather primitive with an upright rod on each side by which you adjusted the height of the earpieces. He was fiddling with something that resembled a piece of grey shiny stone. Wires were everywhere.

"Wireless!" he shouted, as though we had all gone deaf. "Cat's whisker. Damn and blast!"

"Wonderful!" said my mother, as though he had invented it. "Wireless!"

"What?" yelled my father, lifting one earphone.

"I said *Wireless*," my mother called back.

I did not understand why it was so called since wires were so much in evidence, but willingly took my turn to experience the new marvel. The earphones, which I found obscurely repulsive, were clapped on, cutting you off from life; then into the dreadful silence of deafness came a crackle, a hideous scrape and suddenly, far away, a frail voice said *Hullo-hullo!*

"Is it a telephone?" I asked.

No. It was far more strange, almost frightening; yet soon we had cast off our fears, were fighting to have a turn. The earphones were detached from their metal arch and we stood, one a-piece, listening while Dad manipulated the cat's whisker, evoking the rifle-shot crackles, the faint voice.

"Think!" said my father. "What this means! The world's greatest orchestras in your own drawingroom! Music from any part of the world!"

"Wonderful, wonderful!" carolled my mother.

His vision exceeded ours. We asked no more than the Hullo Man and his little songs about Naughty Peter Rabbit; but like the boat and the gramophone, the new toy could only be enjoyed in my father's presence. During the day it was locked in his room, safe from our heavy-handed jabs with the cat's whisker.

"Of course," he said as we squabbled over the earphones—which were always too high or too low, and slid up and down or reversed themselves against your ear—"of course eventually these won't be needed. The sound will come direct, amplified."

We looked at him blankly. Music to come from that crystal? Impossible. Yet so conditioned were we to his infallibility that we believed him.

My father kept his professional life apart from ours. We never went to his office and the only clients we ever set eyes on were those who were also friends, and thus came to dinner, or were somehow involved with boats. But though the Law was sacred there were occasional incidents which could be shared with us. These, usually concerned with cranks and lunatics, gained in telling from my father's sardonic wit and were enormously successful.

When he was interviewing witnesses for the *Greycliffe-Tahiti* case a man appeared in his office, announcing himself as star witness for the Union Steamship Company, which owned the liner *Tahiti*. He claimed to have seen everything and to be able to prove the accident was the fault of the ferry *Greycliffe*.

"Where were you?" my father asked.

"I was on board the *Greycliffe*. I saw the whole thing. I could see it coming. The ferry went straight at the *Tahiti* ...."

"If you were on board the *Greycliffe*, and were not drowned, how did you get ashore after she sank?"

"When I saw the collision was coming I jumped. I jumped aboard *Tahiti*."

"The ship is very much higher than a ferry-boat. How did you manage to jump up to the deck?"

"I am an expert jumper. It was no trouble to me."

"Well then, if you jumped aboard *Tahiti*, how did you get

off her? She did not stop to set down passengers, she went on out to sea."

"As we were leaving I jumped down into the pilot boat."

"And how did you get off the *Captain Cook*? Can you produce evidence that you went in her to Watson's Bay?"

"I didn't go to Watson's Bay. As we passed Camp Cove I jumped ashore."

My father said, "All this is most interesting. I wonder would you be prepared to show the court how well you can jump? Perhaps you would jump for us from the floor into the witness box?"

"The feller wasn't very pleased," my father told us. "He went off to the other side and offered to prove to them that *Tahiti* was responsible for the collision."

My mother, describing herself as a Stay-at-home, was a vicarious gadabout, a gatherer of crumbs. When her family went anywhere she must be told all about it—what people ate, wore, how they looked and behaved. Parties must be described in detail, précis of plays or films given, conversations repeated. Sometimes her sisters would deal with her questions impatiently:

"How was the Garden Party, Ame?"

"Oh, as usual. Ada Holman's hat blew off, of course."

Nothing annoyed her more than such offhand replies and since nothing pleased me more than a chance to describe, embroider, invent if necessary, she and I were in full accord in this matter.

"What happened at Aunty Amy's party?"

"Everyone talked. It was all Bosh Bosh Bosh."

"Don't use that word, Nancy!"

I did not know the word was spelt Bosch. I said, injured, "But they did. The Bosch chair and who's going to get it."

"Ah! And what did Ame have on? Did Uncle Launce sing? What did you have to eat? Was Mildred Muscio there? Went to school with her—Mildred Fry—pale little thing . . . long fair plait down her back. Terribly Clever, of course."

We would draw it out for hours, I would act, impersonate, she would laugh and exclaim and marvel and criticize. She was a wonderful audience, listening to every word, questioning and prompting at any signs of flagging; but the practice was not without hazards.

"What did Uncle Albert do?" my mother once asked, after a lunch at Nan Tay's.

I said innocently, "Oh, he put on his glasses and peered round for the salt."

She was very amused. She told Jemima, who proudly told Uncle Albert.

"Only six! Such observation!"

Uncle Albert, who was shortsighted, did not see the joke; he saw only impudence. He complained to my father, my father complained to my mother and she, who had laughed and said, "How like Albert!" reprimanded me very severely.

The Creaghs were all cool for months.

As we grew older our attitude to our mother became a mixture of defensive secrecy about our own affairs, amused tolerance, protective affection and conniving conspiracy. Though she tried to keep up appearances we knew she was unsophisticated, a muddler, no good with money, easily cowed. When the aunts were inclined to bully her—*Really Flo! Eating chocolates at Greek tragedy!*—we attacked on her behalf, but did not hesitate to laugh at her ourselves for her gullibility and timidity.

Constantly expecting burglars, especially when my father was out, she always communicated her fears to us. She would slide noiselessly through one's door in the dark and whisper tensely, "There's someone downstairs!" Woken thus from sleep it was easy to panic.

When we felt brave enough we would go to investigate in the attics with a cavalry sword. We would put on all the lights and clump about noisily, talking loudly to sound like a great many people. We would fling open the drawingroom door and, shrill with nerves, cry, "Come out, I know you're there!" and in the sinister answering silence John would thrust with the sword under arm-chairs and sofas whose tired springs nearly touched the floor.

Sometimes the alarm was, "There's someone trying to get in!" At these moments my mother would cleverly trick the intruder into thinking there was a man in the house. While we cowered in our beds she would call bravely, in a loud voice, "George! George! Wake up George, there's someone at the door!"

There was no one called George in the family, except a second cousin once removed. We were mystified; so was my father, when one night trying the office key by mistake he heard his wife's voice, loud and strange, in the darkness of his own house, commanding George to wake up.

My father's lofty attitude to money had strange effects on his family. Though we lacked nothing we never at any time had pocket money or allowances, even in our teens. When our aunts commented upon this feudal subservience my mother would tell them to mind their own business; if one of us questioned our dependent position we would be accused of ingratitude.

"Ungrateful girl! How can you! You have everything you can possibly want!"

These restrictions gave us a peculiar attitude to money. We grew up penny-wise and pound-foolish. Though from our mother we inherited the belief that money is to be spent and enjoyed while it lasts, my sister and I still feel guilty about certain kinds of expenditure, no matter how small. I am un-inhibited, even unbridled, about travel and other so-called luxuries yet hesitate to take taxis, or sleepers in trains. These were considered the last word in decadence and self-indul-gence and, like telegrams and long-distance telephone calls, were associated with extreme emergencies and desperate measures.

As financial dependence gave us a lopsided idea of money, my mother's refusal to let us have front-door keys created further complexes. Though able to set out without hesitation for the most far-flung foreign country I cannot visit across the street without feeling guilty if I come in late.

"Why do you need a key?" our mother would ask. "We never had keys when we were girls. There is always someone to let you in."

Yes; but who wanted to be let in, coming home at all hours from a party? She could not understand this at all. She could not rest, she said, till she knew we were in. She would lie awake waiting for the police to ring and announce our death in a car crash, tossing and turning and getting up and making tea till she reached such a ferment she exploded when we appeared.

"At this hour! Like a *servant girl*! I haven't had a wink of sleep! If your father *knew* . . . ."

She did not realize that our father knew. Many times he let us in at dawn, a book in his hand, having read the night away. His only comment was "Bit on the late side, isn't it?"

Two items of my father's code were *Never go cap in hand to anyone*; and *Never touch time-payment*. Though these excellent principles come easier if you have never lacked money or influence I believe he would still have maintained them if he had been underprivileged and impoverished. My mother, on the other hand, would have defied both if she had dared. She was constantly threatening—behind my father's back—to go and see or write to some prominent friend to further someone's cause. She never did; but she once had a fling with time-payment.

"Dad has seen so much *misery* caused by these wretched time-payment sharks," she would obediently tell us, seeing enticing advertisements in the paper, and would sigh rather longingly. She was a sucker for bargains, special offers, every cheap swindle put out by unscrupulous advertisers, for men at the

door, fortune-tellers, raffles, lotteries, sweepstakes. She guiltily
bought materials from itinerant "men off a ship" (*Don't tell
your father!*), surreptitiously took tickets and often won—
hams, handbags, fivers, even £100 in a Tattersalls Sweep. She
could win on chance; we had to win, if at all, on skill. This
was the basic difference between Creagh and Mack blood . . .
the ant and the grasshopper.

"Sheila! Nancy! Come and see!" she cried excitedly one
morning, with a note of fear in her voice.

A high-pressure salesman, one foot in door, was brainwashing her about an Electrolux. By the time we were half-
way downstairs he had pushed her back through the hall into
the drawingroom.

"Take a seat, Mrs Creagh," he said hospitably. "I'll give you
a demonstration."

She sank, hypnotized, into an armchair while he plugged
in the unwieldly barrel and ran the rigid pipe to and fro over
the carpet.

"Look at the dirt!" he said accusingly, opening the apparatus
and emptying out a sackful of dust.

My mother looked stricken and guilty. She said weakly,
"All that dust could not have come from this carpet."

"You'd be surprised how much dust a carpet like this can
hold," he said sharply. "Without you suspecting it."

"I'm sure . . . ."

"Think of your family! Think of the danger to their health!
The germs in this *filth* . . . ."

She looked indignant at the word *filth*. She knew she was
being duped; but the salesman mowed her down suavely.

"In a Gentleman's Residence of this size you must have
many fine carpets to look after. A large area. Take the staircase, for instance. Upstairs bedrooms . . . ." He made for the
door.

"No no!" said my mother, heading him off from the stairs
—beds unmade, things on the floor, dust, *filth*—"There is no
need to go upstairs."

"I'd just like to demonstrate to you . . . ."

"Yes yes, I can see. No need!" And as he moved again towards the stairs, "How much is it?"

"Ah! Let me see!" He brought out his price list, studying it as though for the first time, then made a pronouncement.

My mother, wondering how to escape, said dubiously, "Oh! Well, I don't think . . . ."

He became a shade patronizing, showing even a tinge of insolence.

"Of course, Mrs Creagh, if you *prefer* you could buy on our Easy Terms."

"No. No, thank you. I don't think . . . ."

"Ve-ry easy. We can suit *anyone*. For instance, we have many ladies in the—ah—less ex*cluz*iv suburbs who avail themselves of our special *low* instalment system. If you prefer, of course, I could suit you in *this* category . . . ."

Flustered, guilty, overpowered, conscious that Sheila and I were goggling, my mother gave in. As soon as the bully had gone, promising to come back next day for The Papers, she turned to us.

"Well!" she said defiantly, even arrogantly. "So now we've got an Electrolux!"

We were not much help.

"Ooh!" we said. "What's Dad going to say?"

"I really think I'm entitled to some little comforts at MY age!" she said aggressively; then, uneasily, "Of course, with such small payments I could do it out of the housekeeping."

"But doesn't Dad have to sign The Papers?" Sheila reminded her.

Sign the papers! It was lucky he did not tear them to shreds.

"Send the thing back!" he commanded. "Have you gone out of your mind, to buy at the door?"

"But dear, it's quite a *good* Electrolux. It's quite *new* . . . ."

"If you wanted one of these machines I'd have given you the money. Send it back!"

"But dear, I've paid a deposit."

"You had no business to! I'll give you my cheque for the rest and you will post it immediately! Immediately!"

"He's coming tomorrow. The Papers . . . ."

"Papers! Sharks! Give him the cheque when he comes and tell him not to set foot in this house again. I will not have people of that sort hanging round the place! I will not have this sort of thing going on!"

My mother was very brave when the bully returned. Flanked by Sheila and me she addressed him coldly.

"My husband has left a cheque. We prefer not to engage in time-payment," she said, and shut the door quickly.

The Electrolux, unwieldy, complex and enormous, remained. I cannot remember it ever being used.

14

Night on the Harbour

Out on the frosty lawn I fidgetted, waiting my turn at the telescope. There was a telescope on the balcony at home, through which my father monitored the sailing techniques of others; this one belonged to our cousin Alan Mackerras and was for looking at stars.

The sharp night stung my cheeks; the stars sparkled very white in the moonless dark. It was cold, I longed to go inside.

"Betelgeuse . . . Aldebaran . . . Bellatrix . . ." said my cousin's quiet voice. "Antares . . . ."

My fidgetting stopped. The names: the *names*!

". . . Antares, the most beautiful star in the sky. The red heart of the Scorpion."

The Mackerrases were scientific, Ian a medical researcher, Alan an engineer who loved mathematics and astronomy. Science, my mother and aunts had always inferred, was the arch-enemy of poetry; but what was this if not poetry?

I stared up, bending my neck back, while Sheila spied through the telescope.

"There's the Scorpion. You can see him just over the house, standing upside-down with his tail curving over his head . . . ."

I saw him. He was clearly recognizable, unlike the frustrating Southern Cross, the sketchy Orion's Belt. Glittering, in magnificence he hung above the dark chimneys, lashing his tail.

"Do you see his heart? The red star . . . ."

The red star glowed angrily, beautifully through the darkness. Sheila was asking a question.

"Just good luck," Alan said calmly. "If the earth were closer or further away from the sun, life as we know it could not exist."

"But who put us here?"

"It happened," he said, like a yogi, a Zen master. "It is."

No one put us here; no one. It just happened. We are. And we are no more important than ants. Such enormous loneliness, such shattering insignificance should appal. Disposed to whimper, I looked up at the dark dome, the pinpricks of light. I breathed the scent of early pittosporum, saw the bare young arms of the wintry trees. The Scorpion shone bright, his body of spaced-out jewels, his glowing heart. I felt I might die of such beauty. Lonely? Who could be lonely in such a world?

And in this world, life was lived through the senses. Sounds, scents, colours, light, warmth flowed unimpeded into one's being and one was part of it all, an extension. It was enough to take in the warm privet-scented air of summer, feel the soft damp sea-mist on the face; to watch the midnight moon drawing vapours up from the bay, to wake in the dark and hear water washing gently round rocks, the deep far-off endless sigh of the sea sucked into submarine caverns.

In that summer world, sleep was an involuntary interruption, night no mere negation of day but an entity in its own right. Soft, scented, luminous, full of its own faint sounds, darkness revealed beauties too subtle for daylight. At night I prowled in the garden, climbed on the glistening roof, went to the beach or even further afield. Often I went out to watch the sun rise, lowering myself by a rope from my balcony, though it was easy enough to leave by the front door.

Easy to leave but hard to get in again. You had to climb over the balcony wall and hope that the drawingroom door was unlocked. In the hall, still warm from night, I would stand listening, pierced afresh by the vulnerability of a sleeping house—the faint easing creaks of old wood, the diningroom clock, a swooning benighted mosquito, the vibrations of unconscious breath—then furtively climb the stairs to my room.

It was not enough to see the bay at night; I longed to be on it, at the mysterious hours when the stars sank down and the tide turned and strange forces were abroad. Since my parents would not have approved such marine nocturnal communings with nature, and since *Mrs P. Kirby* was kept in the boatshed at The Spit, I had to wait for this freedom till I got a canoe.

Though despised, this was tolerated by my father—at least it had no engine—and was kept on the beach. Free of boatsheds, dinghies, moorings and a need for wind it could be taken out at any time and though 12 ft long and built of cedar could be dragged single-handed across the sand.

Sometimes with John, often alone, I let myself over the balcony and crept to the beach. Fearful of sharks in the dark water round my ankles I pushed off and hastily stepped aboard. Launched on a glittering sea I set out towards the Heads, where the sleeping ocean gently breathed.

Off Grotto Point, paddles at rest, I floated, blanched by the moon. The encircling hills were black against the sky, shadowed beaches dark triangles of mystery. Where the beams struck, wan crescents glimmered, pale and forlorn. Far off the lights of a ship climbed up over the edge of the shining plateau.

Behind the beauty was menace. Slowly, slowly, as I dreamed and gazed, the frail canoe drifted, moving sideways towards the shadowed sea where the bombora drew you down to the depths. I heard the lonely cry ringing out, saw the gurgling death in the moonlight. The paddles flashed, throwing off brilliants as I hastened away, fear heightening the night's enchantment.

We were used to harbour festivities. Every year my father was vice-chairman and honorary secretary for the Anniversary Regatta Committee and we went on board the flagship, a large decorated ocean liner. A special launch came to Cremorne

Point to fetch us; brass bands played Gilbert and Sullivan, starting guns went off, we lolled in deckchairs watching the races and ate fat afternoon teas. My father, rather flushed from the official luncheon, was briefly glimpsed among the hierachy.

But this was a special occasion. A warship was bringing the Duke and Duchess of York to Sydney and private boats wishing to see the landing must be early in position in Farm Cove. We were to take the boat from The Spit, leaving at some unspeakable hour and proceeding under power—a remarkable novelty in itself.

Friends who were coming with us stayed the night to be early on hand but we were all too excited to sleep. My mother was up half the night preparing food and thermoses. Towards four o'clock our father summoned us. To allow for mishaps on the way (he distrusted engines) he decided we must leave The Spit at five. Those who demurred were reminded that they were going to witness History.

History was a glimpsed pink hat with pink feather-duster at one side. Among cheers, sirens, hooting ferries, the Royal launch swept down the lane of dressed yachts and was gone. Unable to leave our allotted positions we turned to food, to while away the hot morning. Meanwhile the Premier, Mr Lang, was greeting the Duchess in *sandshoes,* our scandalized Aunt Alice reported from her seat in the official stand.

The edges have run together now, the long bright day on the harbour, the flags and sunburn and fireworks and tired-happy-irritable coming home; but the setting-out is not blurred.

Hustled down to The Spit with our baskets and hats and loyal flags we stood on the boatshed pontoon waiting to be taken out to the moorings. There was no marina, no club-rooms or restaurants, only the dark sour-smelling interior where mosquitoes whined among boats on chocks and men relieved themselves through floorboards in secluded corners. The Moreton Bay figs glistened with nocturnal dews and no breath stirred their heavy leaves. Though licensed to be abroad at this hour, voices were lowered. The boatshed proprietor's children, eyes stuck with yellow sleep, came rope-haired and ruffled to gape and sniff. My mother could see immediately that they never had cold showers or even went in for a Dip.

The tide was high. Water lay over the float and halfway up the pontoon, so still, so pellucid that no submerged outlines wavered. Shoes had better be taken off, in case. Jellyfish careened slowly past, almost brushing bare feet. Did those adenoidal boatshed children realize their luck, to live here, so close to it all?

"All aboard!" commanded my father and the first boatload, handed in with squeaks, set out across the smooth sea. Waiting on the pontoon for my turn, my throat constricted. Why did one feel so strange at such times? Anticipation, happiness, joy, yet a vague despair. To be there was happiness; but how to share it, receive it back from others, as the water mirrored the yachts? Would it always be like that—incomplete, just out of sight, beyond reach? Could words ever communicate?

Now the coffin-shaped *Mrs P. Kirby* was back. The rowlocks creaked as we slowly moved into the silence, the stillness. It would be a scorcher, my father predicted, himself dressed for the North Sea, with red kerchief round his neck and salt-stiffened waistcoat lashed on. A white mist lay low on the water, concealing sheltered coves, blotting out familiar head-lands, holding and dampening sounds.

"Cast off!" said my father. The mist receded before us, fainted, rose in wisps and vaporized into air. Half-invisible, we glided down the stream, past pallid beaches locked in noc-turnal trance, trees dark and gravely withdrawn. Gently the boat's white nose parted the pale sea. Slanting ripples ran back from our sides. We were an arrowhead moving through liquid space.

The despised engine, since there was no wind for sailing, allowed complete indolence; the early hour, the absence of witnesses permitted lying face-down on deck, gazing over the bows.

Through the mist came sounds, Italian night-prawners

returning home, Portuguese fishermen making for Pearl Bay; then a faint breeze lifted our limp burgee and we were crossing the open bay below our house. Under the red roofs on the hill people were still asleep, we said proudly, as we ate sausage rolls and bananas. Only we were awake.

But beyond the tide-marking headland, past the swell of the entrance, the Sow and Pigs light, we were no longer alone. From misty corners of Manly, Balmoral, Clifton Gardens, boats were setting out, joining the white armada, dressed with pennants and streamers, crowded with summer people, hastening towards the rendezvous. There was an air of picnic, the sun blazed down on the sea, the air vibrated with engines; voices called and laughed and now ferries appeared, taking landlubbers to their viewpoints. Bradleys Head, Cremorne Point, crawled with coloured figures; ships at anchor were hung with flags. Beautiful, young, gay, the morning sparkled in blue perfection, robbed of all magic, all mystery; no longer my own.

15

Lady Authoress

ONE day my mother came home from Nan Mack's rather late, swept into the house, began dramatically: "What do you *think* . . . ?" but could not wait for our guesses.

"Your Aunt Louie! Louie's back! THERE I was, SITting on the verANda when I heard someone coming up the steps. I thought it was Alice. I said, 'Is that YOU, Alice?' And WHAT do you think? A voice said calmly, 'No. It's me. Lou!' Isn't it *typical*?"

We were stunned. It was hard to believe we were to see this aunt, so long a legend, so briefly remembered, so often discussed, the dazzling intrepid adventuress who had written her first book on the corner of the washstand, starved in a London garret, dashed off dozens of novels, been wrapped in sables, lived in an Italian villa, escaped from the Germans, come back like a heroine, acted like a princess, then vanished without a word and not been heard of for twelve years.

"And that's not ALL!" said my mother, stunning us further. "She's got a NEW HUSBAND!"

A new husband! We hadn't even seen the old one, dead long ago, so they said; the delightful mysterious Dublin barrister they all spoke of so fondly, so evasively that we could only suspect a Failing.

Sheila said, "What sort of husband?"

"A CHARming New Zealander! An Anzac! We'll meet him tomorrow night. They're coming to Nan Mack's for dinner."

The next evening we went nervously with our parents up to Jemima's. The grown-ups were drinking sherry in the drawingroom. In the hall was a short woman in a black lace dinner-dress, with dyed hair and a made-up face at which we stared. (Our mother, who had a beautiful skin, never made up.) She looked at us critically, smiling, friendly, amusing, alert; but where was the delicate flower-like baby face, the blue eyes and golden curls of legend? The foreign glamour? She was *old*! She was not exotic, not even different; in fact she resembled my mother.

But only in looks. As soon as she spoke, in a soft, dove-like voice, I felt again the old discomfort of the long-ago panto-mime matinee. She was charming, charming but she was laughing at us, at everyone, especially Sheila and me.

"Little Osstrylians," she said. "Have some kyke?" And while we smiled gingerly, "Do you know, I met one of the mistresses from your school. I asked her if you were pretty. What do you think she said?" And in perfect imitation of a well known voice, "'I wouldn't say they were *pretty*, but they have Bright Intelligent faces'!"

In the drawingroom where Jemima sat enthroned, uncles and aunts were gathered round a tall slender good-looking man.

"This is Allen Leyland," said Louie. "He's an Anzac! Allen, these are my little Osstrylian nieces. They Lyke Kyke."

Allen, Sheila and I exchanged glances of mutual embarrass-ment. We sensed, he well knew, that Louise spared no one. Everything served her as material, for writing or a clever saying, like her beloved Mr Archibald of the *Bulletin,* who, she would tell us, swore he would have used his sainted mother for copy.

The Leylands moved into a house on the North Shore Line and

our Aunt Amy's troubles began. In no time Louise was at work among her sister's friends, beguiling them, winning their hearts, ridiculing them behind their backs, a custom that did not remain secret for long.

"Ame's got so *smug!*" she would say scornfully. "So suburban. All those Bod professors' wives."

"Louie's imPOSSible!" said Amy, exasperated. "And it's extraordinary how she gets hold of such nice men!"

Allen was gentle, humorous, *simpatico,* delicate. He had been gassed in the war and developed T.B. We grew to love him; nor, despite our aunt's unpredictability, could I resist her charm.

Her house was exciting in a way quite different from Amy's. A bottle of wine on a red-and-white checked tablecloth, garlic, *risotto,* chicken *cacciatora* were exotic after my mother's wholesome home-cooking. Louise talked all the time she cooked her Italian food, of Florence and Paris and Katherine Mansfield, of J. M. Barrie (*Such a MEAN little man, I lived next door to him in London, so hatefully MEAN with money*); of D'Annunzio (*His villa was near mine at Settignano, outside Florence. Like a little cock-sparrow ... three hundred pairs of shoes ... the most beautiful actress in the world—ah, Eleanora Duse—adored him and he treated her vilely*); of du Maurier (*Ah, how I loved him! When* Trilby *came out* Punch *said he had invented a new style they called "Wegoism" ... "Come along with me, Reader, you and I together!"*); of Lily Langtry (*Like a tired snake*); Isadora Duncan (*Such a bore!*). She recited Italian poems, impersonated Tuscan *contadine,* German landladies, Australian society hostesses, Chairmen of Committees (*Miss Louie Smack ... Speaks for herself!*). She was funny and clever and ruthless, full of sparkling malice, splendidly lacking in reverence for convention, the Establishment, the whole bourgeoisie.

But there was always the feeling the weather might change. She would grow bored and cantankerous if you crossed her. To go out with her was alarming. You never knew what she was going to do or say or command you to carry out. Any reluctance caused disgust and scornful words. For her, other people's sensibilities seemed not to exist.

She soon became a source of mixed pride and terror to her family. One never knew when she would swoop, how she would behave. My mother would shudder to see her hypnotizing simple admirers at parties.

"Mrs Creagh, your sister is completely *charming*!" the unsuspecting victim would say. "And she's promised to dine with us on the 15th . . . ."

"I wish they wouldn't, they wouldn't!" my mother would moan. "If Louie takes a dislike to them . . . you KNOW what she's like. I WISH people wouldn't make a fuss of her! You know what she *does*—ridiculing them behind their backs!"

It was all very well for my mother, but what about us, at our schools, helpless, exposed? Louise had embarked on Travel Lectures. With the cachet of the Education Department and the Better Films League she was whirling from school to school, addressing the pupils, inviting them to patronize her matinees.

"I was just coming out of Robson's study from getting a Saturday!" John roared with indignant misery. "And I ran into Louie! She dragged me back in with her and said to Robson, 'Do you know my nephew John?' as if she was introducing us at a party. The Old Man said sarcastically, 'Yes. We *have* met!' "

"God!" said our athletic cousin, Harry, also at Shore. "She said to Robson, 'Do you know my nephew Harry? His father, my brother Gus, came here too.' " When Robson said there were hundreds of boys in the school and he didn't know all their christian names, she said, 'Oh, but you must know Harry! *He ran a mile!* "

We held our breaths when she came to address our school but all went well and there was a brief reflected glory after she talked to us in Assembly.

"We're going to Travel-travel-travel-travel-*travel*!" she promised; and sure enough we did, marched off with the Shore boys and Redlands girls to a local hall where she showed her films and talked and did impersonations and played the piano and enchanted her audience.

For years after, learning that Louise Mack was my aunt, contemporaries would confide, "You know, it was your aunt who first interested me in travel. When I was at school I went to one of her lectures and never forgot it."

Some of her family never forgot those lectures for different reasons.

"This scene shows Indian boys, sewing," announced our aunt from the platform. "Of course, most Australian boys don't sew, do they? But some do. I know one who does. My nephew, Jim Pilcher! He sews because he's a Scout. Scouts can sew . . . ." and when the embarrassed titters had died away: "Jim! Are you there, Jim? Is Jim Pilcher in the audience?" Stepping up to the footlights she commanded, "My nephew, Jim Pilcher!"

At the back of the hall where the Shore boys were sitting, a significant silence descended.

"Jim!" called Louise sweetly, firmly. "Will my nephew Jim Pilcher please stand up?"

Prodded by friends, Jim rose, angry, scarlet, embarrassed.

"Is that you, Jim?" The whole audience was now craning its necks, girls tittering, boys guffawing and shuffling. "Jim, come up on the platform and sing!"

Louise soon decided that I was to be a writer and though at this time I thought I might be a musician or a singer or even a doctor, set about brainwashing me.

"Pianist! You don't think YOU could ever be a pianist? Look at your hands . . . look at your tiny hands. How do you think you could play the 'Emperor' with hands like that? Singing? You've got a voice like a screech-owl. You'll never be any good at music. You can't play. You can't sing. You're wasting your time. Medicine? You couldn't pass those exams. But writing . . . ah, writing! Don't you want to Live? Don't you want to Travel and See the World?"

I wondered silently why only writers Lived, Travelled, Saw the World. It seemed to be their preserve.

"Shut up in a room playing scales all day. That's not LIFE! But writing—you can write anywhere, any time, in any part of the world. You only need a pencil and paper. You're always writing. When you tell me about the people you see in the tram you are *writing*. Don't you know that? Writing isn't just sitting down at a table in front of a paper, it's people . . . life . . . things happening. Lying in bed at night thinking about people you've seen, wondering about them, making up stories about them . . . that's writing! Why do you want to be one of those BORING singers screaming arias? You go now and write me a story! Go on! Go and start work at once, you lazy little beast, loafing down on the beach all day!"

Overawed, I obeyed. The story was acclaimed, I was to be taken to London immediately. I was to starve, to suffer, to *live*!

"Nonsense!" said Aunty Amy. "Don't take any notice of Louie! She'll take you to London, then lose interest and abandon you. She does that. She's no good example. She had talent, she started well but she never would work, never would take any trouble. Slapdash. Undisciplined. Always rushing off to the ends of the earth. Don't you listen to her. You just go on as you are, doing the washing up and one day you will find you have Something to Say. And if you have Nothing to Say, for God's sake don't write."

"Ame doesn't know what she's talking about," said Louise. "You must go out and see Life. You must have Experiences. It's all very well for her, she's not a novelist. She only writes about birds and flowers. Those fearful Bod articles of hers in the *Herald*! That's not Life. Life is the little woman up at the shops, the sick child, the cry in the night . . . . That's Life!"

My father's form of encouragement was rather more practical.

"If you're going to write you'll need a Roget and a Bartlett," he said, handing over my grandfather's calf-bound, miniscule-printed *Thesaurus* (1855) and a fat blue book of quotations and classical allusions with which to embellish my forthcoming works in the approved elegant 18th-century manner.

Not only were Louise and Amy each other's sternest literary critics; they were also too different in temperament not to clash. In some ways Amy's protected life with Launce had made her timid, while Louise's endless battles had strengthened her. Amy now preferred to recollect in tranquillity; Louise was still in the thick of it all.

In general, my mother got on well with Louise, no doubt because Flo never argued. Sometimes there were enchanting hours when they exchanged reminiscences, partly for their own pleasure, partly for ours.

"Do you remember . . . ? Do you remember at Newtown? At Redfern? Do you remember *Narani*? Do you remember *Quamby*? Do you remember that Bod young man who wrote in the Album . . . ?"

"Do you remember, Lou, when you sent your first poem to the *Bulletin* and signed it M. L. Mack?"

"And Mr Archibald wrote me a letter saying, *Dear sir*!"

"And asked you to go and see him."

"And I went six times and was too shy to go in. And at last I went in and upstairs. And Mr Archibald was expecting a man!"

"Instead of a Pretty Little Girl in a Simple White Dress, with golden hair and blue eyes."

"And a fringe and an innocent expression, which was all the rage at the time."

"How good Mr. Archibald was to you, Lou!"

"Ah! He was an Angel. And he took me under his wing and encouraged me in my writing. Do you remember, Flo . . . *Up in a corner—always in a corner, gentle and dreamy . . . .*"

"Your poem about Mr. Archibald!"

> *"Two brown eyes shining,*
> *Shining with kindness,*
> *Shining with wit, but shining with kindness . . . .*

Ah, he was an angel. *Up in a corner, holding a pen.* How he loved writers! His cupboards were stuffed with manuscripts he had bought. Did he ever use them all, I wonder?"

"Then he gave you that job!"

"And I wrote the Sydney Woman's Letter, for three years!"

They would laugh and sigh and wipe their eyes and start again.

"I always thought A. G. Stephens was sweet on you, Lou."

"Ah!" A mysterious sentimental simper. "But he was very good to me about my poetry. Do you remember, Flo, when he published my book of poems? . . ."

"*Dreams in Flower!*"

". . . And wrote the Introduction . . . ."

". . . And said it was the Most Distinguished Body of Verse written by an Australian woman!"

> *"Oh Garden, garden! Yes, evermore,*
> *Awake or sleeping, or passed or passing*
> *The secret gateways of Death's domain . . . ."*

> *"My heart shall haunt thee for joy thou lost me;*
> *My soul shall search thee for vanished pain."*

"*Dreams in Flower!* Ah!"

"Ah!"

More sighs.

"Remember, Lou, when you wrote *The World is Round*, on the washstand?"

"And sent it to London?"

"And Fisher Unwin accepted it. And I thought I was made!"

Listening, we could identify everything, everyone. It had all been told us or we had read it in Louie's books. We could pick out the people and incidents from *Teens*, *Girls Together*, *The World is Round*, *Children of the Sun* and match them with their sources in real life. The chair propped up with the log; the apples that weren't enough to go round; the girls, late every morning, keeping the tram waiting; the horrible guard who turned Lou (Lennie Leighton) off, the day she lost her ticket and poor Aunty Alice (Floss) tried to squelch him by saying, "*Guard, what is your number?*"

We knew it had all happened, that our Aunt Amy (Brenda) had walked through town dripping wet with her shoes in her hand after being capsized; that Louise had eaten the Head-mistress's lunch and run a school magazine in competition with Ethel Turner. We knew that *I'll tell my big brother. He's a barrister and that's almost a policeman!* had really been said by Herbert Curlewis's little brother and that it was Louise's own elegant suitor who insisted on carrying her parcel, un-aware it contained a leg of mutton and a sheep's head.

"Do you remember, Lou, going to see the sun rise?"

We knew this story by heart, not only from *Teens* but from constant re-telling. In the book the girls, staying at Blackheath, in the Blue Mountains, set out with their mother's permission at 5 a.m. to watch the sun rise over Govett's Leap. In reality they crept out at two o'clock without Jemima's knowledge.

"Remember Maggie, Lou?"

They both giggled. Maggie was a little girl they had met at Blackheath.

"Lou thought it would be nice to ask Maggie to come with us, so she took us to her house and knocked on the front door."

"*You* were scared, of course."

"Of course, I was always timid. But Lou, it was two o'clock in the morning!"

"They were all asleep, snoring their heads off."

"So Louie threw a stone at the window."

"Then Maggie's mother opened the door. She had her hair in curlers. What a fright she looked!"

"It was *two o'clock*! She said, 'What do you want?' And

Lou said calmly, "*Is Maggie In?*" At two o'clock in the morning!"

"I just asked if she would like to come with us to see the sunrise. The woman was very rude."

"She was furious! She said, 'Like your impudence! Go home at once, you naughty little girls!'"

"But we did see the sun rise, didn't we, Flo? Over Govett's Leap. It was worth it!"

"Yes. Over Govett's Leap. Oh yes, it was worth it!"

Sometimes they talked of the days in London.

"I was giving a party, a very smart party," said Louise. "All the most interesting people in London. And Alice had just arrived from Australia."

"She was so *pretty*!"

"But so dowdy! I looked at her and said, 'You'll have to get a new coat. Have you got enough money?' And Alice said, 'Oh yes'. Then I said, 'You'll need a new evening dress', and Alice said, 'All right'. I said, You'll need this and that and so-and-so', but whatever I said, Alice said, 'All right'. So I finally said, 'Alice, have you *really* got enough money for all these things?' and she said, 'Oh yes, I've got plenty'. I *looked* at her and I said, 'Alice! How much *have* you got?' And Alice said, 'I'VE GOT THIRTEEN POUNDS'!"

"Poor Alice! She thought it was a fortune. So it was to us, in those days."

"So Alice got a new dress and came to my party but when she saw all the elegant people she felt very shy and didn't know what to say. She went and sat on the window seat with a quiet little Chinese gentleman. She thought he looked rather shy too and she had better try and make him feel at home. So she said . . . ."

Pause; then my mother burst out:

"*'You seenee St Paulee Cath-ed-er-al?'*"

"Be *quiet*, Flo! You're spoiling my story! And do you know who he was? HE WAS THE CHINESE AMBASSADOR!

An Oxford graduate! A famous scholar who spoke FOUR-TEEN languages perfectly, including English!"

And together my mother and aunt would shake and wipe their eyes and crow happily, "You seenee St Paulee Cath-ed-er-al!"

16

Holidays

THREE times a year we went away for school holidays. Though we lived by the sea we were taken each summer to Palm Beach, to Newport or Austinmer. In winter we went to the Blue Mountains or the Southern Highlands.

Our father joined us at weekends. He marvelled at my mother's enthusiasm for exchanging a comfortable house for a furnished cottage with few conveniences and several extra children to feed.

When I first went to Palm Beach with my Aunt Amy there was no through road. We took trams to The Spit, to Manly, to Narrabeen, then a primitive bus over terrible roads to Newport harbour and a launch across Pittwater to Palm Beach, landing at Gow's Store, below *Four Winds*. The journey took hours but it was beautiful. I can still remember Pittwater that day, the utter calm of its surface in great heat, the faint low mists through which you glimpsed shining satin that stretched on and on. The hills were untouched and silent and the sound of our launch echoed round us and back as we moved.

Palm Beach was still a sparse settlement when we began to go there each year—a few doctor's houses on Pill Hill, a few on Sunrise Hill and one or two round the harbour. Down on the flat towards Barrenjoey were campers. Though my mother loved Pittwater because it was like Italy and my father because of sailing, they both had a phobia about Westerlies and the Afternoon Sun, which meant we must always face East, like Moslems, and suffer bracing sea winds and freeze when the day was cold and not have a view over Pittwater.

Life was simple and unsophisticated. When not on the beach we were plodding up hills in the heat. No Intellectuals stayed with us, though Amy sometimes came for the day and once or twice brought our dear Professor Woodhouse, in a tussore suit. Wiping tea from the underlining of his moustache he said with gentle petulance, "I'm not going past Angus and Robertson's any more. I'm sick of seeing *Lasseter's Last Ride*!" It was hard to believe all those orange books in A. & R.'s window had come from our Mr Idriess, *Ianthe*'s silent rope-coiler.

We had no car and if we had my mother could not have driven it; but we had A. J. Hordern, a friend of my father's, with an Edwardian beard and Edwardian tastes. He doted on us and wished us to call him Uncle Alfred, but though we were fond of him *Alfred* was just one of those names.

He would rush up in a big square car like a hearse, full of ice creams and watermelons, and drive us wildly all over the peninsula. Although his fortune came from a famous city store, he, like Mr Lloyd Jones, seemed exempt from my mother's condemnation of Rich Shop-keepers. Was it because they didn't stand behind counters, wearing aprons? Or was Rich Shop-keeper really a state of mind?

A.J. so loved Palm Beach he decided to build there for himself. He chose a large green hill in the far corner above the beach and since it was feared the owner would put up the price to match his resources the land was bought for him in sections by others. On it he built a beautiful house called *Kalua*, with white columns, facing the sea. Though American in influence, the garden was South Seas, with palms and hibiscus. Mrs Hordern, a dark fat lady with soft eyes and voice, came from Hawaii. This house is now considered to be worth a fortune.

There were still a few of the old Palm Beach identities, like the Hitchcocks, our landlords for some years, who formerly kept the dairy. Mrs Hitchcock was a stout old lady with a tiny shrunken head, a yellow face puckered round insecure false teeth like petrified ticks. Thin hair, barely hiding the scalp, was dragged back into a hard little cumquat-sized knob. Her voice was a shrill jagged screech.

Mr Hitchcock, a dear, slow-spoken, mild, portly, ruddy and amiable country man with white moustaches, was chivvied along by his garrulous wife. Their new house (*"Bod!"* said my mother) on the Ocean Road, was full of weird ghoulish photographs hoisted up near the picture rail. Someone's ashes were kept in the frigid parlour.

Mr Hitchcock was used to driving a sulky and when he bought a car seemed never to realize it would not stop if you said *Whoa!* He liked to take us for drives and though my mother was always nervous she hated to hurt his feelings and would sit miserably in the back waiting for the catastrophe. She did not gain confidence from the fact that he was learning to drive from a book, which he consulted as we moved along, while Mrs Hitchcock, her little yellow death's-head topped by a black straw boater, sat in the front, helping find the right page.

"Just a minute, we'll see what the book says," Mr Hitchcock said calmly, as the car rolled backwards towards the cliff edge at Whale Beach. "Find the page, Mother."

Mrs Hitchcock ruffled the pages and said, "Put on the hand-brake, it says."

"Now, which is the handbrake?" her husband pondered; but my mother had wrenched the door open, pushed us out and was jumping herself.

"Quick, quick, Mrs Hitchcock!" she cried in panic. "Get out, get out! It's going over the edge!"

"I'm staying 'ere!" Mrs Hitchcock replied in her eldritch screech. "Where 'e goes, I go!"

"Ah!" said Mr Hitchcock, unaware of the commotion. "This 'ere must be the brake"; and he applied it.

During the week we surfed on an almost deserted beach but as time passed and the road from Narrabeen was built lorries came at weekends, bringing people and beer. We saw little of them for my father was down from town and our lazy beach-comber life changed. We surfed very early and spent the rest of the day in strenuous walks to the lighthouse at Barrenjoey and expeditions across Pittwater to Scotland Island or the Basin or other remote beaches.

Barrenjoey was inhabited by a lighthouse-keeper's family and a few goats. There was only a rough steep track and you had to scramble and crawl over stones and crevasses. The view at the top, though magnificent, was rather frightening. As we stood, hot, scratched and panting among those formidable rocks my father would wave at the Manly ferryboat taking day-trippers to Broken Bay.

"There they go! Out for a Two-bob Spew!"

The marine excursions were more to my taste. Pittwater was like an old family friend. My father had been sailing boats to Broken Bay all his life and coming down for Pittwater Regatta since its inception. He loved every part of this then uninhabited inland sea; but at times my mother's love for it was overweighted with terror. Though she had absolute confidence in her husband she had none in the boats we hired from Gow's shed, which she scornfully called Little Cockle-shells. She was always uneasy when my father, who enjoyed this form of aquatic slumming, rowed us about the open stretches of Broken Bay.

Her fears were not unjustified. One day a storm blew up and the cockle-shell sprang a leak. My father rowed on, showing no signs of perturbation while my blanched mother, in the stern, clutched the infant John to her breast. Sheila and I baled with a pie-dish. It was really perilous, the little boat was low in the water, very old and porous, but my father got us home safely, spurred on perhaps by the thought of so ignominious an end for a yachtsman.

I never doubted his power to save us in such situations. Far more frightening, in a quite different way, was the beach at The Basin. Secluded, completely deserted but for a broken-down hut, it seemed sullen, even ominous. There was a sense of mangrove-swamp horror, claustrophobic and threatening. Its sands were strange. When the tide went out hundreds of soldier crabs emerged and marched menacingly, the silence horribly broken by the faint scrambling whisper of their advance. I was terrified at the thought of being left behind there, the very hint of shadows beginning to fall brought panic. Reason could not lift my fears. Something had happened there, long before my time, evil vibrations still lingered. The others seemed unaffected and I was ashamed, but I never could escape quickly enough from this beautiful poisoned place.

My mother loved the Blue Mountains. Not only were they intimately connected with her youth, she genuinely enjoyed the cold, the endless walks, the bracing winds, the yawning abysses and primitive weatherboard cottages full of draughts and Austrian chairs. Though I liked the fun of friends staying, the giggling in double-beds, the big meals and roaring fires, I could never accept the wind, the cold, the ugliness of the buildings, the hostile landscape, the dry parched air, the spiky aggressive bushes. I also resented the ceaseless call to action— *Don't sit there with a book . . . go out for a walk!* The only experience I really cared for and chose to retain from the Mountains were the green smells in neglected gardens. In this frigid climate grew plants and flowers I rarely saw at home: primroses under hawthorn hedges, holly-trees with red berries; snowdrops, crocus, lily-of-the-valley, hyacinths, bluebells. Daffodils thrust green snakeheads out of a frost-hard earth, unfolded their smooth leaf-sheaths beneath aromatic Blue Mountain cypress and pine.

These flowers were more delicate and reserved than those in our garden, more timid yet more resolute; and the smells were different. At home, warm and close to the sea, flowers gave themselves too easily, spent themselves all at once. Stocks and roses were heavy with scent, petals like coloured velvet quickly softened and fell. They had a perishable beauty that made me sad without knowing why; but the mountain flowers, embalmed in their arctic atmosphere, remained crisp and cold, fragrant and beautiful; nor did they droop and wilt but withered up quickly, cleanly, in the dry ruthless air, leaving only their juicy-leafed sheaths.

They had a secrecy, an intimate kind of exclusiveness. You had to squat right down to see the snakeheads coming up or find the buds among the primrose leaves. Most mysterious of all was the smell of the slender-growing bulbs. If you sniffed with eyes shut all was greenness, smoothness, coolness. By some strange process scent became colour, a degree of temperature, a texture, a tactile and visual experience; your fingers felt, without touching, the cold matt sheaths, your closed eyes saw dark moist earth and sage-coloured spears.

My father shared my dislike of the cold. He only came at weekends when, perhaps to keep warm, he would march us at a great pace through the Passes and up and down cliff-faces where only a broken rope protected you from ghastly depths. He never permitted dawdling or gazing. Sometimes in the depths of a valley there would be smells of damp earth, the chill clarity of a stream, sparse shafts of light through shifting leaves, furtive movements of birds and cold little mists round the ankles; but you were not allowed to enjoy them. On, on, to the Weeping Rock or the Bridal Veil, Minnie-ha-ha Falls or Nelly's Glen. It may have been that he was as anxious as I to get it over.

My mother did not come with us. Her idea of a walk, for herself, was a gentle saunter along a level road smelling of pine-trees. While we stormed the Passes she remained at the top with the picnic. One morning, at Wentworth Falls, my father took us and our friends to get water for the billy, while she spread out the lunch. About half-past five we returned, by bus, from Katoomba, having walked the Federal and National passes, taking turns to carry John.

My mother, clutching her heart, said, "I thought you were all dead! I thought you had fallen over the cliffs!" But her only reproach to my father was, "*Really*, dear! Do you want to *kill* me?"

I hated the Mountains; I loved Palm Beach; but there was one holiday place apart from all others, in my mind.

As a boy at Elizabeth Bay, my father had a friend called Alan Pain, son of the rector of St John's, Darlinghurst. After the war, Mr Pain, who was born at Cobbitty Rectory, went back there as rector himself, of St Paul's church. He had married my mother and father; years later he married both Sheila and John.

At Cobbitty, we stayed at *Pomare*, a large old house near the church. Across the road was the Rectory, Gothic Revival, with carved barge-boards, rambling garden and beautiful trees. Mrs Pain was English and tea on the lawn was rather English too. Like the Prayer-book lessons at school, the memory was useful when I lived in an English rectory.

To reach Cobbitty you went by train to Campbelltown, then by steam tram across to Narellan and from there by sulky to the village. It was not—and is still not—very big: a post-office that sold liquorice straps and sugar-balls that changed colour and little mauve musk-tasting lollies; the church and churchyard smelling of sunwarmed cypress; the Rectory and a few low-built cottages smothered in vines. Some were neat and had garden-beds edged with brown-glazed tiles like Hovis loaves and eschscholtzias and primroses and other faint frail flowers among roses and cabbages; some were overgrown, with sagging veranda roofs, broken window-panes stuffed with sacks or papers; cracked walls and ceilings exposed lath-and-plaster.

In one of these lived a witch, a poor whiskered old woman in rags who shouted threats when she caught us peering fearfully in through gaps in the hawthorn hedge.

It was not what one did at Cobbitty so much as what one felt: the hot stillness at midday, the fine white dust powdering the hedges, the smell of cypress in the sunny churchyard, and another smell I could not name but which meant *very old*. Yet though we looked uneasily at neglected graves, swearing we saw bones and skeleton feet, there was nothing macabre. The atmosphere was so serene, so reassuring that I often lay in the high weeds among the graves, watching the sky behind the church spire.

The church itself was rather cold inside and dark and musty. On Sundays we went to hear Mr Pain preach and Mrs Pain play the organ. This was a strange Mr Pain. At other times he was funny and made us laugh; but Sunday lunch was a consolation. The food at *Pomare* was good, especially a miraculous pudding with cold chocolate blanc-mange inside hot sponge-cake.

Beyond the village was the bridge and the river, where she-oaks shaded the grassy banks and great tangled roots lay in brown pools. The river was always cold, and, since it was freshwater, you could only swim very slowly. Here and there were tadpoles and sometimes white violets with purple hearts, growing round mossy trunks.

Across the hills, through deep winding lanes, lived another friend of my father, called Mr Downes. Though I was a small child when I first saw *Brownlow Hill* the simple low Georgian house must have printed itself on my mind . . . its columns and flagged verandas, shutters and stone-flagged hall, its huge separate kitchen and lake with stone urns and creepered walls. Going back as an adult, after years overseas, I found I had forgotten nothing.

Though restored since my childhood, the house is the same. Its atmosphere is unchanged, its beauty increases with age. Edgar Downes, my father's contemporary, now lies in Cobbitty churchyard with his father and grandfather but his son and grandson are still at the old house, where the family have lived since 1858.

Alexander Macleay, the Colonial Secretary, built *Brownlow Hill* for his son George. From its rounded-off hill-top it looks out over brilliant green fields where Friesian cows graze. Ancient olives gone wild, pines, firs, Chinese elms, monkey-puzzle trees surround the hill like a moat. A Georgian aviary of red hand-made bricks, all arches and vines, stands at the end of the rose-garden, beyond the sundial. In summer the old house is a cavern of coolness; in winter, the black shapes of bare trees along deep Devon lanes stand out against low-lying mists. Time, in this rich sheltered place, seems never to move.

17

The Warren

At Hunters Hill lived a family of cousins we did not often see. The long land-and-sea trek from The Spit via Circular Quay was one good reason but there was another, dimly discerned from snatches of telephone conversations between my mother and aunts.

"Oh! The little wretch!" "Oh, she deserves a good *whipping*!" "Poor Sid! Poor Sid!"

Hearing such outbursts, Sheila and I would hang about eavesdropping for it meant excitement and drama. While we, with our other cousins were being brought up rather strictly, the cousins at Hunters Hill were having the time of their lives.

"Kitty! She's spoiling those girls! Allowed to do just as they like!"

Kitty was the wife of our uncle, Sidney Mack. Though infrequently seen she was one of our favourites; dark with shining black eyes and an offhand, rakish elegance. She was always gardening, standing on ladders to paint ceilings, driving the car with a handsome fur coat flung round her like an old blanket, a cigarette hanging from her lower lip. She smoked incessantly, kept odd hours, gardened at dawn and seemed never to disapprove of young people. Born before her time, she was too refreshing, casual, unconventional, honest and real for her period, with her overalls and cigarette cough.

her tolerance and dry quiet wit.

My mother was fond of this sister-in-law but felt uneasily, with the other aunts, that Sid should have a more conventional wife. The wives of other barristers helped their husbands by going into society and entertaining the Right People, instead of messing about with gardens and hens and beautiful old houses.

"Poor Sid! He comes home from a Hard Day in Court and there's no *rest* for him. Those Girls . . . racketing . . . all hours of the night. Kitty!"

"Mind you, Alice, I *like* Kitty. But *I don't think she gives him enough to eat!*"

"Do you know, Flo, that he often has only a *meat pie* for dinner! Kitty's out driving the car for Those Girls. Taking them to parties. Making a Slave of herself for them!"

"He needs good, plain *home* cooking . . . ."

The Meat Pie for dinner was rather bewildering, since there were a cook and a maid at *The Warren*; nor did the delightful Sid show signs of ill-effects or seem any less fond of Kitty. An ambitious conventional wife would not have done for him at all. Erratic, brilliant, off-beat, his absolute lack of self-consciousness sometimes led to strange situations. It was said that during a speech in the Sydney Town Hall he took out his top teeth because they were hurting and put them in his pocket; that one day, mislaying his overcoat, he wore Kitty's fur coat to town. He did not care about the Right People; he liked gay congenial company. At *The Warren* drink flowed, visitors surged in and out, hangers-on abounded, so the aunts said.

"When I THINK," my mother would say, "that Sheila and Betty were born on the SAME DAY!" And she would look complacently at Sheila, so safely enclosed in black stockings and navy tunic while That Betty—precocious minx—was trailing suitors three times her age. Betty, especially spoilt because she was delicate, was a law unto herself. She had a governess, she had a horse; she went into town and bought what she chose, so we were told, and put it on Poor Sid's account. She did not want to go to boarding-school and when she was sent, got herself expelled. The headmistress, censoring mail, objected to letters to boy-friends, particularly those that said, "For God's sake come and get me out of this bloody place."

Though Bet and her elder sister Jess were said to do awful things, to cause their poor parents such *worry*, they all seemed affectionate and happy together. Sid and Kitty were devoted to their pretty daughters, so amusing and wild and full of Irish charm, and the girls returned their love. It was a cheerful household.

All the Macks were bound together by savage tribal loyalty. No matter how much they might fight or disapprove privately, they were united in public. Because Sid was a brother, Sheila and I were sometimes allowed, at the risk of corruption, to stay at *The Warren*.

To go there was thrilling, even the journey. You took a ferry from Circular Quay, then changed at Valentia Street to a very small boat for Tarban Creek. The service here was so informal that our cousin Charlie and his friends were allowed to steer and passengers were often navigated up the stream by boys in Sydney Grammar boaters.

Leaving Valentia Street you entered another world. Pale stone houses, grey slate roofs showed among trees; gardens, lawns sloped down to the Creek. The tranquil afternoon light on that secluded backwater did not belong to the Sydney we knew, to our open-air life at home. There was a different smell in the air, of ancient trees and flowering shrubs, of grey stone sunwarmed walls, old gardens and moss and wistaria, the scent, the mellow richness of slow summer evenings in Cornwall, on quiet creeks of the Helford River.

The Warren stood on the banks of Tarban Creek and its grounds went down to the water. Secluded umbrageous stone steps descended to a boatshed and swimming-baths. After our crystalline beach and rock pools these baths were rather frightening, dark and sinister, undisturbed by tides. There was the sense of something dangerous and slimy in the obscure depths; you dived in with panic and got out as fast as possible, yet with far more excitement than on our wholesome beach. The boatshed was shadowy and secretive in a disquietening way; it hinted of forbidden doings and had a damp, rather sour marine smell.

To reach *The Warren* by land you drove over Fig Tree Bridge and down a dead-end called Wandella Avenue. Inside the gates—always open—was a tall pine-tree and nearby, among jasmine and oleander, an ancient two-seater lavatory, an agreeable setting for conversation. There was a circular lawn, an immense magnolia, Moreton Bay figs and Kitty's camellias; then the house itself, an architectural melange, hung round with creepers.

From the circular lawn you could see the original convict-built house, low and simple, like *Brownlow Hill*, with flagged verandas, slim columns and shutters; but the slate roof had been raised for upstairs bedrooms, with dormers and mullions and balconies never envisaged by the first architect. A porch with tiled floor and scented vines faced the drive; there were long screened verandas, a servants' back-stairs, window-seats, all wrong for the classic simplicity of the old colonial building. They made an exotic jumble to the eye and mind of a child; so did the furnishings—a mixture of elegant antiques, striped wall-papers, portraits of ancestors, new utilitarian objects, bedroom walls with rose-covered trellis, fox masks, stag horns, and a grandfather clock in the hall.

At the back, adjoining the house, was The Cottage, the original kitchen, with two-foot stone walls and stone floor and a baker's oven in the wall. Above was an attic or loft like a belfry, where the youngest Mack sister Pat and I spent a great deal of time. Our attics at home were not like this, stale-smelling, stifling in summer under the low steep roof; they were bigger, they looked out on the sea. You did not have to climb from the landing window across the slates to enter them, nor did they contain trunks and boxes of love letters. Pat and I went ruthlessly through these records of her sisters' love lives, reading aloud the more torrid passages, shrieking with triumph at finding familiar names.

Jess had turned the old kitchen into a little sitting-room with white-washed walls; and here, crouching over the fire with the wind howling outside, she would frighten the life out of us with stories of *The Warren* ghost. All the girls swore they had heard it, rustling and sighing on the stairs. Some even claimed to have seen a shadowy female form. How could we know, as we shivered and squeaked with pleasant chills, what the ghost was telling those doomed sisters? At that time the house was full of young life. In the warm scented nights, lights shone down on the river, voices echoed out over the lawns. Music sounded, people came and went, doors banged, cars drove off. There were laughter and screams of excitement and the girls calling their brother—"Boy! Boy!"—commanding him to drive them, to run an errand, to pick up a friend from the ferry. When Pat and I took our mattresses into the garden to sleep we lay looking up at the stars, the dark beautiful shapes of the trees against the sky, drowsily listening to the gaiety, breathing the scents of magnolia, jasmine, wistaria.

Uncle Sid was a criminal barrister, which we took to be some sort of crook. In fact, in his student days, he had, with my father and Judge Curlewis, perpetrated a felony which never failed to delight us. This incident was resurrected in the Sydney press forty years later.

Sid was plagued by a crowing rooster next door and when stones, complaints, appeals had no effect the three friends decided to kill it. In order to commit the crime with the minimum of law-breaking they tied a cut-throat razor to a clothes-prop and tried to manipulate it through the fence.

"It wasn't easy," my father would tell us. "We couldn't get hold of the bird, it kept running round squawking and we were afraid the owner would wake. Curley wouldn't let us go over—he kept saying, 'It's trespass, it's breaking and entering with felonious intent'; but Sid climbed through and held the fowl. We still couldn't manage the clothes-prop so in the end I went in too, while Curley stayed on the other side, keeping watch. I restrained the prisoner while Sid performed the execution."

We were too young, in our uncle's heyday, to be interested in his work, but two of his celebrated cases were known to us. Jane Smith had been accused of poisoning her husband for insurance money and Sid got her off. Some years later she reappeared, charged with poisoning another husband. He got her off again, but advised her not to rely on him for the third time.

At our kindergarten I had made friends with a pale fragile little boy and his elder protective sister. They were Different because they had no mother at home. She was away "in hospital" and they lived with their grannie. They seemed to cling together, rather sadly outside our noisy activities.

"Poor little boy, bring him home," said my mother, and when he came she was especially kind to him. She was furious when Nan Tay told us with ghoulish excitement, "Their mother's not in hospital. She's in the lunatic asylum. She shot her lover dead and if it wasn't for your Uncle Sid she'd have been hanged for murder. He got her off on insanity."

"Kitty! Kitty! Where's my eye-glass? For God's sake, where's my eye-glass?" Uncle Sid going off in the morning. "Kitty . . . Kitty . . . Where's my teeth? God's struth, where's my teeth?" He sounded so fierce and people said he had a terrible temper, but I always remember him laughing.

"You're a witch, Nancy Creagh. You've got green eyes. I'd have had you burned at the stake a few hundred years ago if you'd come up against me in court!" Screwing in his monocle, he would scrutinize me with his own sharp, clever, kind, humorous eyes.

"Do you really know burglars and murderers, Uncle Sid?"

He would roll his eyes and grind his teeth and say, "All my clients are *Innocent*!" then carol with fiendish relish, "And many a burglar I've restored to his friends and his relations!"

He would prance to the piano and pound out Gilbert and Sullivan, Beethoven sonatas or absurd comic songs.

"Sing 'The Frenchman', Uncle Sid. Sing 'The Frenchman'!" And in an accent no Frenchman could ever produce he would sing:

> *Ven I first kom 'ere from Paree,*
> *I do go to Leicester Skvare.*
> *Take a small room, oh so jolie!*
> *Right up on ze top of ze stair.*
>
> *Tra la la-la. Tra la-la.*
> *Tra la la-la. Tra la-la.*
> *Bon bon! Bon bon!*
> *Tra-la-la-la-la-la-la-LA!*

Swaying from side to side, eyes sparkling, monocle falling out, he raised his hands high from the keys like a mad musician and rolled his *R*s like a French-Tahitian; then his voice became rather mincing and high and he pursed his lips prissily:

> *In ze next room vos a laidee,*
> *On ze piano she play . . . .*

—glissades up and down the keyboard—

> *Music charmant, o so lofflee,*
> *And she sing too, all ze day . . . .*

Very arch and ladylike:

> *Tra la la-la. Tra la-la.*
> *Tra la la-la. Tra la-la.*
> *Bon bon! Bon bon!*
> *Tra-la-la-la-la-la-la-LA!*

Occasionally Sheila and I went to stay with the girls at their holiday house near Cronulla. I remember a lawn, a large rambling bungalow with latticed verandas, Betty's horse, a boatshed down at the water's edge on Burraneer Bay. There was also an annexe for servants and visitors, which had a macabre fascination. The cook had died there in her sleep.

"Fat Maggie," Pat told me. "Bet found her dead. They took her away in a basket. I saw them."

The thrill of horror was mixed with envy. If a maid died in our house we certainly would not have seen her being removed.

At Burraneer Bay Uncle Sid sang, played the piano, wore old clothes and drove every morning to surf at Cronulla. On one of these mornings the steam tram from Sutherland crashed into his car.

We had never known bad news before. Removed from the scene of action we were told only that Uncle Sid had had an accident, that Gordon Craig, my father's friend, was going to operate. That Sid might die did not enter our heads. In our world one's elders were fixed, like the sun or the furniture.

My mother spent much time on the telephone, saying "Wonderful spirit . . . . Pull through . . . . Mack constitution . . . ."

"Bobby will save him," said my father, who had more faith in Dr Craig's surgery.

"Well, Sid," said Dr Craig, after the operation. "I've put you together again. You're full of silver plates and screws."

From the edge of death Sid replied, "Now they'll really be able to say Mack's got a screw loose."

The Warren has gone, but the pine-tree still stands, old, ragged, upright, like a thin battered colonel. All the landscape has changed, it is hard to find your way. You enter Wandella Avenue from an unfamiliar angle and cannot remember these up-to-date, complacent villas with car-ports and venetians and dabs of iron lace.

By a new double-garage, gate-posts lean in a fragment of stone wall; beyond, rough overgrown land leads to the water.

The gates of *The Warren* were always open, but in welcome. This is mere absence of gates.

I walk in, as though trespassing, searching for landmarks. Behind the ragged pine the faint outline of the circular lawn still endures, with tattered magnolia and Moreton Bays. Here Pat and I lay on the thick springy grass and looked at the stars and heard the music, the laughter, and longed to be old enough to join in.

But where is the house? Not a trace remains. Nothing. It is hard to visualize where it stood. This is a desert, scarred and abandoned; yet as I go on, compulsively, the path grows familiar.

Suddenly, among the weeds, my feet are on the old stone steps down to the boathouse, the sinister baths. It is all fresh again . . . the breath-held excitement of plunging into the dark tideless water, the shadowy boathouse. Near the baths, now full of slime, are two aloes, hacked about, on the stone embankment where you dried yourself. I remember them; and the twisted roots of Moreton Bays, the caves and rocks, now scarred by blasting.

But where is the scent of magnolia, the spreading trees, the convict-built haunted kitchen, the attic-belfry where we read the love-letters? Where is the scrubbed servants' staircase, the drawingroom where Jess entertained her swains in a rosy dim light and Sid sang "The Frenchman?" Where is the diningroom with the big mahogany table with brass claws, the kitchen with the vast revolving cabinet given by "a grateful client"? Nothing left. No sign. No trace of flagged veranda or slatted shutters, no echo of laughter or gaiety.

I look for Kitty's garden, her wistaria, her crumbling old blue-washed wall with the arched doorway and sunflowers and banana leaves, through which she would appear at dawn, with secateurs and cigarette hanging and dark amused eyes. A fresh hard breeze from the west blows down the upper reaches of Tarban Creek and the sky shines with a ruthless blue glitter. It is a harsh beautiful day without poetry. All round, on *The Warren*'s subdivided land, new, split-level, architect-designed Contemporary Homes have survived, sensible, sanitary, sane. They flourish discreetly, in excellent taste, round this elegy where I stand.

"When I can afford it I'll take off all these Victorian excrescences," Kitty would say. "I'll restore the house to its original form"; but jasmined porch and mullioned windows outlived her. Then planners drew a line through the old house, through the Chapel of Ease on the hill where her daughters lay in their coffins, through Mary Reiby's cottage and St Malo, and the bulldozers followed so faithfully that now I stare, bewildered, not knowing where *The Warren* once stood.

In the wilderness is a grove of Kitty's camellias, high and covered with buds. It is astonishingly poignant that they should have escaped, gone on growing without her. Trying to get my bearings from here, from the pine, the ghost of the lawn, I stand wondering. Where was the house? If I could just find a trace, a tangible sign. Nothing. Only the adamant arch of the new Gladesville Bridge overhead, the crumbling stone embankments above the drive, which, in my childhood, were covered with moss and ferns.

Nothing. If I could find *some*thing . . . a fragment; yet it is more than ten years since the house was destroyed.

I look down and through the thin sandy earth at my feet I glimpse tiles. With a strange sense of dread and excitement I scratch and uncover part of a design. Afraid to go on, lest I am mistaken, I pause. Was this really the porch, the deep tiled porch, the threshhold of that gay tragic house? I scratch and scrape again, using twigs and branches; and at last, broken, chipped, full of gaps, here is the red and blue pattern I remember. A little more scratching and a white marble slab shows through.

The doorstep; the entrance to the front door! Now I know where I am. The house assembles itself round me, with its people . . . lovers led over this marble step, brides setting forth, infants to be christened, coffins carried out, people collapsed with grief, shock, horror, despair, helped across. So much life and living, gone without a trace, like the marsh at Ephesus where Diana's Temple once stood.

18

One Summer Night

In the heat of the day, when not on the beach or out in the boat, we lay on the floor. Here, with food and books spread round, you could eat, read, listen to music, drop off to sleep or do nothing, without change of position. The long dining-room was a cave looking out upon water and leaves, and in the drawingroom, though bare legs might stick to the piano stool, high ceiling, pale walls created a shadowy refuge.

Outside, cicadas rattled and roared in parched trees; strips of harsh light glinted under the blinds. In the gloom, the sound of the flute rose, coiling like smoke, up, up, wistful, tender, aspiring, but gently, trustfully, vulnerably. John and I, at one with each other and Mozart, lay face down, flanked by splayed spaniels mournfully enduring our strange inactivity.

If it wasn't Mozart it was Bach. Mozart took you by the hand; he melted away the hard core. Gentle and loving, he sparkled, sang like a thrush though underneath he was lonely and frightened and sad. Bach was security; he explained, made you laugh, made you peaceful, gave you courage and hope. He was never sad, only thoughtful; never frightened.

At night, moonlight streamed over the balcony. The shining path out on the bay had jagged edges, like roughly-cut tin. On the warm stone wall John sat, knees drawn up, leaning against a stone pillar, eyes on the sea. Slowly his hands moved the accordeon.

> *Oh Shenandoah, I love your daughters,*
> *A—way, my rolling river . . . .*

Shadows moved under the vines, the air was heavy with sweet pittosporum, the lanoline scent of wistaria.

> *Tis seven long years since last I saw you . . . .*

The sad song, the mournful accordeon were part of the shimmering night. Across the water a few lights shone; on the grassy flat at Clontarf campers had lit fires, voices echoed. Blanched, glittering, the sea hastened in, towards the dark remote hills of Middle Harbour. Far out, the diamond bracelets with rubies and emeralds crossed the entrance; beyond was the sleeping Pacific. Why should we not believe that summer would last for ever?

Yet it was a summer night when someone knocked noisily on the front door.

"Just at dinner time!" said my mother. "You go, Nancy."

Against the black oblong of the open door stood a black and white figure—Dimsie, in a black dress with a dead-white face. From that face I knew, somehow, that life would never be quite the same again.

"Where's your mother?"

Her voice, like her eyes, was wild and lost. Though her hair was smooth there was a feeling that she had been out in a violent wind.

I seemed unable to speak and Dimsie to leave the front step. Her eyes were enormous. But now the family were edging into the hall. My mother's voice was sharp.

"What is it? Is it our mother?"

In that unnatural unDimsie voice came the most unbelievable name.

"Launce."

"*What?*"

"It's Launce. Launce is *dead!*"

With a loud strange cry like a furious protest my mother burst into tears. Sheila started to sob. John, looking frightened, began to fondle his dog, who all canine prescience, licked his face desperately. I seemed to be without breath. There was a stab in the small of the back, a weird chill moving rapidly down the spine to the final vertebra. I became rigid and cold. No tears, no breath; only a pain in the chest.

Dimsie wasn't crying. She just looked wild and mad. Launce and Amy were down at Narooma, on the south coast. He had gone out in a boat with some friends to fish . . . . Amy was walking along the street when she saw the crowd on the quay. She went up—Launce on the ground—a cerebral haemorrhage —nothing—nothing to be done.

"Oh Amy! Oh, poor little Amy! Oh Amy!"

Why was my mother saying Poor Amy? It was Uncle Launce who was dead! But now she began to say, "Launce . . . Oh Launce! So young!"

"Forty-eight. Only forty-eight," Dimsie said bitterly.

"So young! The prime of his life!"

So young. So *young?* This was something to focus on, to help restore the normality that had suddenly gone, with everything overthrown and grown-ups crying like children. Fortyeight wasn't young; it was decrepitude, an age when any reasonable person might expect to die. But there was nothing reasonable here. The thought which might have led back out of the frightening wood led nowhere. Nothing made sense. They were talking and acting as though our laughing uncle would never be seen again.

Jemima had been told. She had said, "His time had come!" That seemed strangest of all. How was I to know that old age accepts shocks more calmly than youth?

"I must go," Dimsie said. "They are bringing Amy up to Sydney. I must be there to meet . . . spend the night . . . ."

"I'll come in the morning," my mother said hoarsely, and seemed not to notice as Dimsie slipped away.

For a moment we stood, dinner plates awry on the table. My father was not home and we did not know what to do next. Sheila was crying quietly on the sofa, John had slunk off to his room where he wept his bewilderment between Towser's floppy ears.

"Poor Sheila," my mother said. "Her first grief."

I felt suddenly quite alone. Dimsie had gone, John had Towser, Sheila my mother. It seemed frightfully unfair. Did she think that I didn't care because I hadn't cried? Hurt, proud, I walked out of the house and nobody noticed.

In the dark garden I stood pressing my fists against the constricting pain in my chest, thumping from time to time as though to beat it out. Apparently, when this sort of thing happened there was only yourself. I looked up at the stars and wondered where Uncle Launce was, but it was all too unreal, it didn't make sense. It hadn't happened at all, things like this didn't happen to us. Not to *Us*.

Since no one had missed me I might as well stay out. I walked down the rough quiet Parrawi Road to The Spit. There were scents of summer flowers, dust and the sea. Near the Spit Baths the trees on the sand were very dark. A few spindles of light fell, unmoving, on the black water. I smelt seaweed and shells and dimly discerned the pale shapes of moored yachts. I wished I could go out to the boat and never come back.

Yet how silky the water, how golden the long reflections. They seemed to have been laid down carefully on the surface, their edges sharply defined, and beyond, in the blackness, the bay was asleep; no sound but the faint lapping at my feet where I sat on the damp sand. How beautiful it all was.

I realized guiltily that I had for a moment escaped, forgotten everything; but after all, what did it matter? The truth was still there, unmoving, like a great hateful stone. You could look away for as long as you liked and it would be waiting when you turned back.

But no matter how hard I tried, it still made no sense. Uncle Launce's handsome face, his blue eyes and teasing laugh would not fit the context of death. He could never be anything but alive. I tried, childishly, to think of angels in white robes, as Jemima described them, but saw only a funny photograph of him in a white kimono, with his elbow on Professor David's shoulder.

Should I do something to hurt myself as punishment for lack of feeling? But what? I bit my lip, clenched my fists till the nails cut my palms, but no tears came. Again I looked up at the sky but Uncle Launce was as much out of place there as among Jemima's angels. I looked at the stars and thought of him singing the "Requiem". I remembered the sad sad music, the poem that said, *Under the wide and starry sky, Dig the grave and let me lie* . . . but now the words were empty, without meaning. There was confusion and blankness. Only the pain in the chest was real.

"I must go home," I said, through suddenly chattering teeth; but I was afraid. How could I go back to the house where the others were weeping? Their tears could only reproach me; and besides—Out here at least there was unreality. The news made no sense; it hadn't happened. To go home was to see proofs that it had, that the pattern had started to change, the background to shift. It was not grief I feared to face but the knowledge that nothing was permanent any more; that one was always alone, in peril, *exposed.*

19

No Trespassers

In many ways Launce's death seemed to have killed the Amy we knew and loved. Though eventually our aunt moved back into society she was never the same again. The indignant snort was heard more often than the giggle, the smoker's cough was constant. As time passed, grown rather crabby, she took to strange dressing, shawls clutched round the shoulders like Mother Machree.

"Why does she dress like a little old egg-woman?" Sheila asked.

My mother said angrily that we were little beasts.

Occasionally there was a flash of the old personality, the creator of the impudent small birds and fishes of *Bushland Stories*; but often these moods led to tears because they were part of Launce. It was hard to believe this sad little monochrome woman had ever been the naughty adventurous Brenda of *Teens*, had ever signed languishing portraits *Toujours à toi*, or made us laugh at Caruso's *I Caught a Prawn*. Dimsie, who was going away to London again, sighed and said that Amy had died with Launce.

My mother and Alice conferred in long telephone conversations.

"She shouldn't stay there alone. It's *unhealthy!*" "She ought to go on with her writing." "She ought to have an Interest."

"She ought to adopt June or Barbara . . . ." "She ought to sell the house . . . ." To please her sisters, at first, Amy had a series of university students to live, for company. We did not appreciate their great brains nor they our juvenile charms. When we stayed with Amy, who now didn't get up till late, we had to breakfast alone with them. We were glad when she gave them up.

We still went to Gordon but increasingly "to help Ame". We brought her morning tea in bed, cooked, did chores, weeded, went to the Village for shopping. The house always seemed empty, for all its books and Persian rugs and antiques; even when people came there was the feeling of absence. Launce's caps, stick, pipes, books lay about as though he were expected back any minute. The sittingroom echoed silently with his beautiful voice.

I knew now what it meant to miss him; that people don't die in one brief announcement. There had been a great funeral with the Premier and all kinds of eminent men; the papers were full of notices, articles, tributes to his work, his world reputation, his services to scientific institutions. They meant nothing at all. The only reality was the stillness that hung over the house at Gordon. Where Launce had once stood smiling was only a space in his shape; where he had sung and laughed, only silence.

> *Tirra-lirra*
> *By the river,*
> *Sang Sir Lancelot . . . .*

Grief did not draw Amy any closer to Louie; she found her sister more provoking, more impossible than ever. Louie felt Amy lacked courage and said so, frequently. She disapproved of Ame giving up writing, of the way she was letting herself sink into old age.

Though life was not easy, Louise was far from defeated. No matter how exasperating, she was always alive and stimulating, with her bravely dyed hair and weird theatrical, sister-in-law shaming clothes. Having insulted most of her sister's university friends and quarrelled with all the North Shore matrons she had moved to our area. Amy, busy patching-up, smoothing over in her own district, wore an expression that meant, "Now you'll know how it feels".

Louise took a house overlooking Middle Harbour and called it *Villa d'Este*. She did this wherever she lived, whatever the house, even small brick bungalows in back streets. This *Villa d'Este* at least had a view but was perilously close to us. My mother began to quail.

"She's made mischief between Alice and Elsie S. . . . ," she told Amy regretfully. "After all these years . . . ."

"How cruel!" said Amy complacently. "Alice's *one* friend."

"Louie is naughty!" an uncle's wife said plaintively. "I had all these women for bridge and she turned up, dressed like a wild gypsy and began to find fault with their playing. They'll never forgive me."

"Really, Louie is *too* bad," said Louie's old friend, Zara Aronson. "She said 'Surely you're not asking Charlie Lloyd Jones to your party? He's only a draper!' "

Even my mother was not spared.

"The trouble with Flo," Louie confided to Flo's friends, "is she's so mean with food. She doesn't give you enough to eat." Nor was Flo consoled by knowing herself a by-word for lavish providing.

Life had become all vendettas, plots, court favourites and intrigues. The family grew to dread Louise's uninvited appearance at any gathering. At parties she would lure Sheila and me into corners and murmur clever destructive comments, intended for overhearing, upon the guests; in smaller groups she would make outrageous statements, mildly, softly, among her family's conservative friends on unmentionable subjects—*Italians make better lovers than husbands*—or hint at fictitious and fantastic gossip . . . (*She went in Mrs Moore and came out Mrs Paramour*). The methods varied, from an elegant wearing-down blackmail before visitors to simple attack; yet sometimes the latter seemed less an assault than the disinterested exercise of a talent, a trying-out of words that took no account of truth or the victim's feelings. "She smiled her sour smile and slid away . . ." was a good phrase even though the subject was known for the sweetness of her expression.

Or was it perhaps done as a protest against her family's treachery? The only Macks who fully retained their old unconventionality to the end were Louise and Sid, and Sid was the one she loved best. Her sisters had, in a sense, betrayed her, grown substantial, settled, even prosperous and, to her mind no doubt, *bourgeoise*; her other brothers had impossible wives. All the sisters agreed on this. Though the brothers-in-law were loved and admired the Mack men were held to have made disastrous marriages, except Uncle Hans, who lived 12,000 miles away.

To retain Louise's approval you had to be prepared to face any embarrassment.

"For goodness sake, Flo," she said at an orchestral concert, "surely you know better than to *ask*! Never ask! They always say No."

"But the seats are all numbered," my mother said nervously. "And ours are over there. These may be reserved for someone else."

"Well, they're not here, so we can use them. They're far better than ours," and Louise settled herself as though the discussion were closed.

"But suppose they come later? It could be so awkward!" and my mother, appalled at the thought of public reproof, timidly beckoned an usher.

"I told you so!" Louise hissed, white with rage as we trooped back the way we had come. "I told you not to ask! You should have just looked as though they were our seats!" Nor did the arrival of the owners in any way lessen her fury.

Since I was the elected writer I had a harder standard to live up to.

"Never worry about what people *think*!" she would say. "Experience is what matters."

I felt this was true but there were times when it was hard to observe.

"It's empty," I reported one day, as we stared at a house marked TO LET. "It's locked up."

"Never mind, we'll go in."

I followed her into the overgrown garden, inhibited by the daylight, the proximity of a busy highway and a notice that said trespassers would be prosecuted.

"Come on, come on! Don't dawdle!"

"It says . . . ."

"Never mind what it says. You musn't take any notice of that sort of thing. Come along, I like this house. We'll go in."

"But it's locked."

"Try again."

"No, it's locked," I said thankfully.

"Try the back door."

Back and side doors were tried, and at her insistence, all the windows.

"It's no good. We can't get in."

"Then you must *break* in!" Louise said firmly. "Go on. You can easily break a window and crawl through."

It was a summer evening; workers streaming past on their way from town had a clear view of our activities. I thought of my father and the police. I said, "I can't."

"Of course you can. You're small. You could get through that one there. Or just break the glass near the fastening and push it open."

I said, "It's breaking and entering. It's breaking the law. We'll be arrested."

Her incredulous disgust was shrivelling.

"I see!" she said coldly at last. "I see! And I thought you were different! I thought you had courage and daring. I knew all the others were MICE; but you . . . . Now I know you're just like all the rest. You'll never be a writer. You're *afraid*!"

From time to time she would decide to polish our Australian crudity with lessons on poise and charm.

"When some one tells you you're pretty or that you look nice, don't just simper or say, 'I've had it for years.'" She mimicked us to perfection. "You should say, 'Thank you. I'm *so* glad you think so'; or 'I'm glad you like it'. That's poise.

"And your hands. Look at the way you hold your hands, all clenched up. No *Frenchwoman* would use her hands like that! Here . . ." she demonstrated a flowery movement. "You see? You and Sheila have *beautiful little hands* and you use them like *washerwomen!* Now watch!" Again the graceful gesture. "Come on . . . ."

We tried. She said, "Nancy, your hands are disgraceful. It's that boat. How can you hope to be elegant if you go out in boats and hang on to wet ropes? Do you think Eleanora Duse did that? Do you think Isadora Duncan, Lily Langtry sat about clutching wet ropes? Now! Come along! *How nice you look!*"

Embarrassed, inclined to giggle, we mumbled, "Thank you."

"How pretty you are! Your hair is ravishing!"

This, being not in the script, brought paralysed silence.

"Well, go on! *I'm so glad you think so!*"

"I'm so glad you think so."

"I *do* like your dress."

"I'm so glad."

"Yes, but don't *giggle*. Smile. Smile . . . not *grin*. Smile like this!" She drew back her lips in what we thought a most affected manner. "No no, not a *grimace*! A smile. There! See? That's poise!"

Charm came next. The first lesson, given at a picnic, was full of surprises.

"To be really charming a woman must know how to flirt."

This was astounding, since we had been taught to repress flirtatious instincts.

"But Mum says . . . ."

"Oh, don't take any notice of *her*. She doesn't know. You

want to be *enchanteresse*, don't you? Then you must know how to flirt. In Europe all men and women flirt. It's a game; it starts in the cradle."

"But Mum always says we shouldn't Encourage boys or Lead them On because while they're still at the university they can't think of marrying."

"Marrying! Who's talking of marrying? Is that all she thinks of? It's nothing to do with marriage. Now watch!"

She leaned out of the car, waved at a rather pompous friend of my father's and fluted, "Mr L. . . . Mr L. . . ."

Mr L. . . . turned in surprise.

"Mr L. . . . I think I have dropped my handkerchief. Is that a handkerchief over there?"

Mr L. . . ., no cavalier, bent and peered at the grass.

"It's a piece of paper, Mrs Leyland," he reproved.

"Thank you!" She drew back and turned to her giggling pupils. "There!" she said triumphantly. "That's a flirtation!"

"But . . ." said Sheila. "Nothing happened. It wasn't even a handkerchief."

"Oh, don't be so stupid! Of course it wasn't. But I attracted his attention, didn't I? I *started something*."

We did not know how to answer this, aware that Mr L. . . . thought her a privileged lunatic.

"But *he* didn't flirt with you!" I persisted. "How can it be a flirtation?"

"Oh, you're so stolid!" Louie said crossly. *Stolid* was even worse than *middle-class*. "You'll never get on in Europe. You'd better stay here with these awful Australian men. You'd better stay here and get *married*!"

When I fell into disfavour, for displaying middle-class tendencies or stolidity, Sheila would be taken up for a nerve-racking stretch as preferred niece, not only carrying out our aunt's commands but being played off against the discarded favourite.

"Who do you think the best looking, Sheila or Nancy?"

Louise said conversationally to her brother Gus.

This uncle, to whom I was much attached, said bluntly, "Nancy, of course."

Sheila blushed and looked miserable. Louise said briskly, "Nonsense!—Sheila's much better looking!"

I doubt if Gus cared either way but roused by his sister's manner he said, "What rubbish! Of course Nancy's better looking."

"Sheila's beautiful. She's like Norma Talmadge. A pocket Venus. I can't *think* how you can say Nancy's better looking. She's *hideous*!"

"She isn't. Look at her skin. Her eyes. Her hair. Her figure . . . ."

"She's got crooked teeth."

"Sheila's too fat."

"Look at Nancy's mouth. It's just like a shark."

With Sheila in tears, my mother flustered, myself stiff with rage, Gus red in the face, the whole afternoon ruined, Louise retired well content. Next week, next day, next hour perhaps the scales would tip the opposite way and I would once more be beautiful, talented, brave and adventurous enough for the supreme privileges of Living and Writing.

20

Sunrise

MONTHS had been passing without sense of time, golden days running together. Each morning I looked out on the glittering bay, the eternal universal dark form of the fisherman in his frail boat, each night fell asleep to the sound of water, whispering, washing the sand.

Yet, there were subtle changes. I had given up smoking and chewing tobacco, went less to the bush and the caves, spent more time with girls at school. Though enraged when teased, I knew perfectly well that the boys who hung about us on the beach were not languishing for John's company; and though pretending innocence, was aware that the youths who rode with their hands on the back of the 8.15 tram were not doing it purely for help up the hill with their bikes.

This discreet but accepted form of courtship was a favourite topic among the girls, second only to Ferrety-face. He was a little man in bowler hat and raincoat, whatever the weather, who travelled in late, empty, afternoon trams. He would fix his petrified victim with pale staring eyes, furtively open his raincoat and reveal himself—"*a saveloy!*" screamed the girls—prolonging the display till he saw the conductor coming. He performed thus for years, since we were all too embarrassed to report him.

Now it was the year of the Intermediate Certificate. For the last ten months, while the other girls worked, I had loafed, swum, dreamed and listened to music. Homework was done on the way to school or not at all; in class, during subjects that bored me, I read or wrote plays with all the best parts for myself.

As the time approached, my parents, who had brought us up to despise Swots, showed they expected me to pass. My mother, who always said proudly, "*I* never passed an exam!" (she never sat for one), my father, the hero of scraping through with last-minute cramming, now chose to remind me that no Creagh or Mack had ever failed in a public exam; that Uncle Hans had matriculated at thirteen.

It was the beginning of summer, with scented nights and tentative currents of warmth in the air. The Scorpion sparkled overhead, but martyred, I now must stay up late, wake early to work. The credulous John was impressed; so was my mother. She crept upstairs at dawn with cups of tea, rather enjoying the drama. It took her back, she said, to the days of *Girls Together*, when Lou was working for the Matric.

I grew irritable, pale, wore a permanent frown, was odiously busy and self-important. No one had ever before been so hard-pressed, so overworked; yet almost subconsciously I was aware that something was going on in the house. I half heard scraps of talk, telephone conversations . . . . "We hope . . . We can't say . . . It's a matter of time. And with Gert away in London . . . hard to know what to do."

"Go up and see Nan Mack," said my mother to Sheila; and when my sister demurred, "I'd *go*, if I were you . . . ." The words hung on the air, full of significance.

"Is Nan Mack sick?" I asked.

My mother looked evasive.

"Oh no, not at all. She's just got a cold."

"Can I go up and see her?"

"I wouldn't if I were you. You might catch it . . . the exam . . . You've got your work cut out . . . . Wait till she's better. Then you can tell her how you got on. She'll want to hear."

Stew-vac. finished; the Intermediate began. In the hot morning light we collected at Fort Street, nervous, excited. Afterwards there were post-mortems, fears and hopes, screams and groans, ice cream sundaes in town at the *Golden Gate* and the ferry trip home. It was fully absorbing; yet in the background persisted the strange uneasiness.

That night at dinner my mother was very pale. Sheila looked frightened. Afterwards, in the hall I heard her say, ". . . it howled all night. I couldn't sleep."

". . . As though it knew," said my mother; then, seeing me, "Go to bed, Nancy. You look washed out."

Dawdling on the stairs to hear more, I said, "I still have some work to do."

"No. Go to bed now and I'll call you *early*. I promise."

In bed, I heard the telephone ring, then murmuring voices; then ringing again. Fatigue overcame curiosity. I fell asleep.

I woke suddenly, in a twilit world, and lay, listening. There was no sound; the house was sleeping; yet there was a difference, something was *absent*. I could hear the bay, down below, the water rustling on the beach. It sighed, then was silent; then sighed again and fell silent again as though wondering . . . hesitating . . . . The sound was familiar as my own breathing, yet this morning it seemed strange.

An absurd incident came to me suddenly: my grandmother ruthlessly squashing her Lady Companion. Poor Miss Smith, always trying to air her culture.

"Aye always think of those beautiful laines of Bayron, which he wrote to his sister, you remember . . . *There is a pleasure in a pathless wood . . . .*"

And Jemima, brutally: "That will do, thank you, Miss Smith!"

It was so vivid, the voices so clear I was startled. Why on earth did I think of that? My brain was keyed up from overwork, lack of sleep. Was I perhaps going mad? At the thought I began to feel queer. I got up and went to the eastern window.

In the ashen light the tide was retreating, flowing out

rapidly, past the tide-marking headland, the lighthouse, the rocks, to the open sea. It was said that the souls of the dying went with the ebbing tide.

At that moment I knew my grandmother was dying, her spirit going out with the grey water, to the ocean that lay, still and colourless, against the wan sky. I knew, but felt no sadness or fear; only calm acceptance.

I went shivering back to bed and lay waiting, and presently there was a sound downstairs. The front door gently opened and shut; footsteps moved down the hall to the kitchen; the kitchen door closed. My mother, coming home. Now I knew why the sleeping house had seemed different; it too had been waiting.

I dozed and woke to find my mother by my bed with a cup of tea. She said, "It's a quarter to five. I promised to wake you early."

It took a little time to remember.

I said, "You're still dressed."

She sat on the bed and said, "I've been up all night. I didn't want to upset you when you're working so hard . . . but you have to know. Nan Mack died about an hour ago, just before dawn. Very peaceful. She had pneumonia. She just slept her life away."

When she had gone downstairs I lay, text-books forgotten. This was quite unlike Uncle Launce's death. No sudden shock; no sadness when I had watched the tide going out, only the peace that Jemima herself must have felt; but sadness now for I had started to understand. I knew now that though *they* die it is *we*, the survivors, who are diminished. A part of us goes with them. With Uncle Launce's, my own death had begun. Jemima's brought it closer. Others would die and each time I would be depleted, though they lived on in me. The *I* that I took for granted was only made up of reflections seen in my family's eyes. When they were all gone, all those who knew *Me*, what would be left? We were leaves blown away in the wind.

Outside, the street lamps had paled, the sky reddened. Kookaburras began, locusts all started up suddenly. At the foot of the hill the daily marvel took place . . . nets, gulls, coloured boats transforming a suburban beach to a shore Ulysses might have known. Far out at sea a diamond flashed as the windows of a fishing launch rose and sank in the swell.

Summer had come, exams were over, holidays ahead. I would miss my grandmother, it would be strange without her, but soon I was singing again, rushing down the hill to the beach, drenched with spray in the boat, climbing out on the roof at night to watch the moon and the stars. Life was good; yet it had changed. People did die; one's family died, it happened to Us. No one was immune; and though the sun shone, the bay glittered and living went on, I knew that childhood was over.